AF840603

ROUTLEDGE LIBRARY EDITIONS:
ECONOMICS AND SOCIETY

Volume 37

TRADE SIGNS AND THEIR ORIGIN

TRADE SIGNS AND THEIR ORIGIN

CECIL A. MEADOWS

Routledge
Taylor & Francis Group
LONDON AND NEW YORK

First published in 1957 by Routledge & Kegan Paul Ltd.

This edition first published in 2026
by Routledge
4 Park Square, Milton Park, Abingdon, Oxon OX14 4RN

and by Routledge
605 Third Avenue, New York, NY 10158

Routledge is an imprint of the Taylor & Francis Group, an informa business

© 1957 Cecil Austen Meadows

All rights reserved. No part of this book may be reprinted or reproduced or utilised in any form or by any electronic, mechanical, or other means, now known or hereafter invented, including photocopying and recording, or in any information storage or retrieval system, without permission in writing from the publishers.

Trademark notice: Product or corporate names may be trademarks or registered trademarks, and are used only for identification and explanation without intent to infringe.

British Library Cataloguing in Publication Data
A catalogue record for this book is available from the British Library

ISBN: 978-1-032-97576-4 (Set)
ISBN: 978-1-041-13599-9 (Volume 37) (hbk)
ISBN: 978-1-041-13608-8 (Volume 37) (pbk)
ISBN: 978-1-003-67059-9 (Volume 37) (ebk)

DOI: 10.4324/9781003670599

Publisher's Note
The publisher has gone to great lengths to ensure the quality of this reprint but points out that some imperfections in the original copies may be apparent.

Disclaimer
The publisher has made every effort to trace copyright holders and would welcome correspondence from those they have been unable to trace.

TRADE SIGNS AND THEIR ORIGIN

by

CECIL A. MEADOWS

Illustrated by the author

Routledge & Kegan Paul
LONDON

First published 1957
by Routledge & Kegan Paul Ltd.
Broadway House, Carter Lane, E.C.4.
Printed in Great Britain
by Wyman & Sons Ltd.
London, Reading and Fakenham

© *by Cecil Austen Meadows*

CONTENTS

CONTENTS

CONTENTS

LIST OF ILLUSTRATIONS

I

INTRODUCTION

THE purpose of this work is to offer a general survey of Traders' Signs as distinct from those of the Inns and Taverns.

Much has been written about the history of Inn Signs to the apparent neglect of those of the Shops.

The writer became interested in the subject while delving into the antecedents of a huge Golden Key which hung above a Norwich ironmonger's shop. This led to a study of other local signs, a series of articles in the *Eastern Evening News*, and finally a broadcast on what had by this time become an absorbing hobby.

The use of Signs and Signboards by traders can be traced back to the early days of the Roman Empire. It is quite possible that both the Ancient Egyptians and the Greeks adopted distinguishing badges or emblems for trading purposes, but little evidence of this can be produced.

In the case of the Romans however, various signs are mentioned in their writings, streets were named after signs, and in the ruins of both Herculaneum and Pompeii actual specimens have been excavated. In the catacombs various trade emblems and tools appear carved on the tombs, which can be regarded as an indication that these same devices were used as signs by their owners when alive.

Little is known for certain about the use of signs until the middle ages, when with the growth and spread of civilisation the trading community began to expand and prosper. At first they chose simple emblems or the tools of their trade for signs, a clear visual indication of their various occupations. The need for signs was apparent in some trades more than others, but when few could read or write some symbol was necessary to distinguish one shop from the next.

As the shops and trades became more numerous, so the variety of signs increased and the choice of subjects ranged far and wide. Often a rebus was used, that is a play on the trader's name, such as a horse fording a stream for Horsford or two or three cocks for Cox. No possible source of material for signs was overlooked, animals and birds, trees and flowers, stars and planets, heroes and heroines, poets and authors, all contributed to the kaleidoscopic world of signs. Many of the devices were taken from the arms of noble families, others from the arms of the Worshipful Companies: survivals of these are still very common among the hotel and inn signs.

Combinations of signs became quite common, some of them ludicrous in the extreme, though there were practical reasons for the joining together of widely dissimilar devices. The apprentice, having served his time, started his own business at the sign of his particular fancy, but he frequently added the sign of his former master to it. In modern times great value is placed upon the goodwill of a business, large sums of money are paid to purchase it on a change of ownership; and similarly in the heyday of Signs considerable goodwill attached to them. A tradesman, moving to new premises in another district, or even a few doors up the street, generally combined his old sign with that of the new shop, even though the latter had been used for an entirely different trade.

A typical example of a queer combination of signs was that of James Maddox, Coffin Maker of St Olave's. He used the Sugarloaf and Three Coffins. The Sugarloaf belonged to a former occupier of the premises who traded as a Grocer, and Maddox added his own device of the Three Coffins to it, making a distinctive but misleading combination.

The signs took many different forms, but most often they were actual models or tools, such as Ploughs, Keys, Gloves, Sugarloaves, Planes, Kettles and many more. The majority of these were gilded both for effect and durability, and were made of wood or metal; if of wood, the ornamental parts were often made of plaster.

The signboards, with pictorial representations of their subjects, were in many cases works of art painted by famous artists of the day. The supporting arms and brackets were fine examples of the smith's art, embellished with intricate scroll work and motifs. In many of the provincial towns the signs were all the work of the same artist, some of whom were more enthusiastic than skilful, but generally the standard was quite high. Errors frequently occurred in the repainting of the signs, particularly in the case of animals and birds, but this was to be expected as many of the travelling sign-painters were unlettered.

The third group of signs consisted of those which were carved in stone or wood and were let into the face of the shop, a practice going back to Roman times, when they were let into the pilasters at the side of the open shop fronts.

As trading grew more competitive the effect was soon noticed in the signs, for they grew larger and more elaborate until in the sixteenth and seventeenth centuries they reached gigantic proportions. The streets were very narrow and winding, and the presence of large numbers of outsize signs made them gloomy, even at midday, for they obscured the very limited amount of sunlight that was likely to filter through.

In heavy weather and wind, these monstrous signs creaked and groaned, and frequently they caused serious accidents to passers-by. Though signs had been compulsory for innkeepers and publicans for centuries, their use had been optional for traders. Charles I, on his accession, granted a Charter to London giving the citizens the right to hang out such signs and signboards as they pleased 'for the better finding out such citizen's dwellings, shops, arts or occupations, without impediment, molestation or interruption of his heirs or successors.'

It can be seen that because the traders had a completely free choice of signs without control, or the necessity for a licence, many of the devices were completely irrelevant, inspired in the main by the desire to go one better than their competitors.

The *Spectator* of April 2, 1710, mentions the use of unsuitable or ridiculous signs. It reads:

> 'I would enjoin every shop to make use of a sign which bears some affinity to the wares in which it deals. What can be more inconsistent than to see a bawd at the sign of the Angel, or a tailor at the Lion? A cook should not live at the Boot, nor a shoemaker at the Roasted Pig; and yet, for want of this regulation, I have seen a Goat set up before the door of a perfumer, and the French King's Head at a sword-cutter's.'

In the words of the Charter the signs were 'for the better finding out such citizen's dwellings, etc.' and however incongruous they were, they still performed the duty of acting as an address until such times as the numbering of streets made them unnecessary.

The following verses from the Roxburghe Ballads, at the time of the Restoration, though referring to Inn Signs, give a good idea of the variety of the signs. They show many of the traditional signs of the period for the different trades as well as some which belonged solely to the inns.

'Through the Royal Exchange as I walked,
Where Gallants in sattin doe shine,
At midst of the day, they parted away,
To seaverall places to dine.

The Gentrie went to the King's Head,
The Nobles unto the Crowne:
The Knights went to the Golden Fleece,
And the Ploughmen to the Clowne.

The Cleargie will dine at the Miter,
The Vintners at the Three Tunnes,
The Userers to the Devill will goe,
And the Fryers to the Nunnes.

The Ladyes will dine at the Feathers,
The Globe no Captaine will scorne,
The Huntsmen will goe to the Grayhound below,
And some Townes-men to the Horne.

The Plummers will dine at the Fountaine,
The Cookes at the Holly Lambe,
The Drunkards by noone, to the Man in the Moone,
And the Cuckholdes to the Ramme.

The Roarers will dine at the Lyon,
The Watermen at the Old Swan;
And Bawdes will to the Negro goe,
And Whores to the Naked Man.

The Keepers will to the White Hart,
The Marchants unto the Shippe,
The Beggars they must take their way
To the Egge-shell and the Whippe.

The Farryers will to the Horse,
The Blackesmith unto the Locke,
The Butchers unto the Bull will goe,
And the Carmen to Bridewell Clocke.

The Fishmongers unto the Dolphin,
The Barbers to the Cheat Loafe,
The Turners unto the Ladle will goe,
Where they may merrylie quaffe.

The Taylors will dine at the Sheeres,
The Shooemakers will to the Boote,
The Welshmen they will take their way.
And dine at the signe of the Gote.

The Hosiers will dine at the Legge,
The Drapers at the signe of the Brush,
The Fletchers to Robin Hood will goe,
And the Spendthrift to Begger's Bush.

The Pewterers to the Quarte Pot,
The Coopers will dine at the Hoope,
The Coblers to the Last will goe,
And the Bargemen to the Sloope.

The Carpenters will to the Axe,
The Colliers will dine at the Sacke,
Your Fruterer he to the Cherry-Tree,
Good fellowes no liquor will lacke.

The Goldsmith will to the Three Cups,
For money they hold it as drosse;
Your Puritan to the Pewter Canne,
And your Papists to the Crosse.

The Weavers will dine at the Shuttle,
The Glovers will unto the Glove,
The Maydens all to the Mayden Head,
And true Lovers unto the Dove.

The Sadlers will dine at the Saddle,
The Painters will to the Greene Dragon,
The Dutchman will go to the Froe,
Where each man will drinke his Flagon.

The Chandlers will dine at the Skales,
The Salters at the signe of the Bagge,
The Porters take pain at the Labour in Vaine,
And the Horse-Courser to the White Nagge.

Thus every Man in his humour,
That comes from the North or the South,
But he that has no money in his purse,
May dine at the signe of the Mouth.

The Swaggerers will dine at the Fencers,
But those that have lost their wits:
With Bedlam Tom let that be their home,
And the Drumme the Drummer best fits.

The Cheter will dine at the Checker,
The Picke-pockets in a blind alehouse,
Tel on and tride then up Holborne they ride,
And they there end at the Gallowes.'

The Great Fire of 1666 destroyed the majority of the old London signs, few were replaced in their original form, and in the seventh year of Charles II, a new Act ordered that signs should not hang across the streets but were to be fixed to the shop fronts. This Act controlled the use of signs for several years, but as time went by it was forgotten and they re-appeared over the heads of the passers-by, larger and more unwieldy than ever.

In 1718, in Bride Street in London, a huge sign collapsed and brought down a large part of the shop front with it. This accident killed four people, as a result of which a commission of enquiry was appointed. The commission failed in its task, no real progress was achieved, but by this time the demand for signs had passed its peak and slowly the need for them departed.

By statute, the signs were taken down and fixed to the fronts of the shops and houses, a process which started in London about 1762, commissioners being appointed to carry it out. The following extract indicates how sweeping the new regulations were and it is easy to see how the whole future of the signboards was affected.

'The commissioners are empowered to take down and remove all signs or other emblems used to denote the trade, occupation, or calling of any person or persons, sign posts, sign irons, balconies, pent-houses, showboards, spouts, and gutters, projecting into any of the said streets, etc., and all other encroachments, projections, and annoyances whatsoever within the said cities and liberties, and cause the same, or such parts thereof as they think fit, to be affixed or placed on the fronts of the houses, shops, warehouses, or buildings to which they belong, and return to the owner so much as shall not be put up again or otherwise made use of in such alterations; and any person having, placing, erecting, or building any sign, sign post or other post, sign irons, balcony, penthouse, obstruction, or annoy-ance, is subject to a penalty of £5, and twenty shillings a day for continuing the same.'

Though numbers had been in partial use since the beginning of the eighteenth century, it was not until the latter part that they came into more general use, and even then many shopkeepers seemed reluctant to adopt them, clinging as long as possible to the old ways. The early years of the nineteenth century saw a rapid decline in the use of signs and signboards by traders and by the middle of it they had virtually disappeared.

Certain signs such as the Barber's Pole, the Pawn-broker's Balls and the Chemist's Pestle and Mortar refused to die. They are still with us, and few Barbers today will carry out their duties without displaying a pole or a modern representation of it.

In searching for evidence of the various signs there are several sources of information which can be tapped, one of the principal being the records of Traders' Tokens. These Tokens were issued by the Tradesmen in the seven-teenth century and were in circulation at the very period when signs and signboards were most numerous.

From earliest years the small coinage of the realm had been neglected, and its very scarcity imposed hardship on the poorer section of the community. During the sixteenth century traders and vintners began to issue their tokens which were made of lead, tin, latten or leather. Together with the abbey counters and various base foreign coins, they made up the majority of the small currency, for the official silver farthings were so small as to be useless for commercial purposes.

This state of affairs remained until 1613 when a patent was granted to Lord Harrington to issue farthing tokens for the whole country. Vast quantities were minted and circulated and on the death of Harrington the patent changed hands several times. In the course of time the patentees refused to rechange the tokens; there existed huge numbers of counterfeits and their circulation was stopped about 1644.

The need for small coins still existed and about 1648 traders and vintners commenced to issue brass and copper farthings and half-pence. These were issued in great numbers until 1672 when the royal farthings and half-pence of Charles II appeared. It is the tradesmen's tokens of this period, the most prolific years of issue, that are styled as Seventeenth-Century Tokens.

The eighteenth century saw a fresh issue of private tokens for in 1754, on account of the vast numbers of counterfeits in circulation, the government suspended the issue of copper coinage. This suspension lasted for more than twenty years and as the shortage of small coins became so acute, private individuals were allowed to issue their own. These remained in circulation until 1797 when the regal copper coins made their appearance and displaced the private tokens.

Some tokens were issued in the nineteenth century, the silver series of 1811 which were prohibited in 1813, the copper series of the same period and the irregular issues of farthings and half-pence between 1839 and 1852 after which no more appeared.

The most detailed sources of information are the Bill-heads and the Tradesmen's Cards, two different classes of material but closely allied.

The Billheads, which give us so much information about the trading conditions of their period, generally showed a simplified version of the actual sign. This was quite natural for the name, address and trading style, as well as the trade itself, had to appear, and the sign itself or its principal motif took second place.

The Traders' Cards, on the other hand, were usually ornate, the sign being shown in a most elaborate manner. These cards, or advertising handbills as they usually were, varied considerably in size, and the many collections of them form the backbone of signboard lore. The task of searching for information has been made easier by two outstanding books on the subject. The first is the *History of Signboards* by Larwood and Hotten, first published by John Camden Hotten in 1866. This work deals with all types of signs, both in Britain and abroad, and is the most comprehensive survey of the subject ever written. The second is *The Signboards of Old London Shops* by Sir Ambrose Heal, F.S.A., published by B. T. Batsford Ltd. in 1947. This is compiled from the collection of contemporary trade-cards and bill-heads in the possession of its author, and is profusely illustrated.

The writer acknowledges the use of invaluable material from these two sources, and for the benefit of students of signboard history a complete bibliography is appended. Much remains to be done, but it is hoped that this all too brief survey may prepare the way for a more comprehensive review in the future.

Before leaving the subject of signs in general it will be well to make mention of a related study, the Merchants' Marks.

Long before the custom of displaying a sign became universal, the need was felt for some distinguishing symbol to be applied to the actual merchandise. When few could read or write it was necessary for the bales of goods in

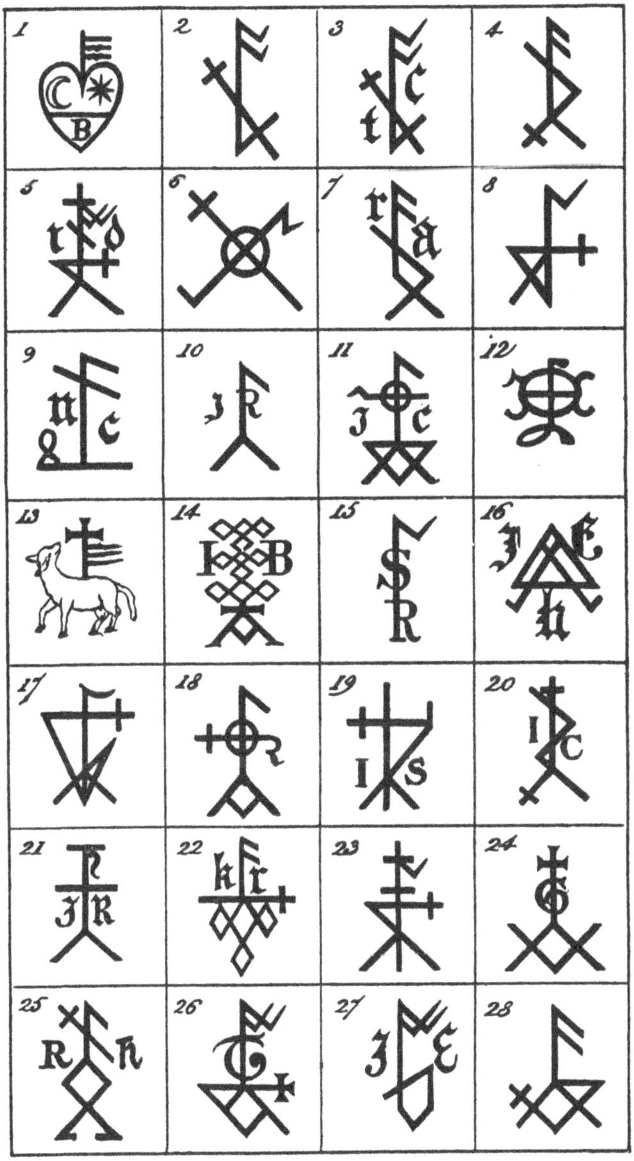

MERCHANTS' MARKS OF
PARISH OF ST ANDREW, NORWICH

transit to be marked distinctively to ensure correct sorting and delivery.

The Merchant's Mark was a private symbol, the forerunner of the present day Trade-Mark, at first quite simple in form and often of a religious character. The cross and banner borne by the Agnus Dei and variations of it were used as well as simple attempts at a rebus of the merchant's name.

There were no fixed rules in the designing of marks but a geometrical basis was common to most of them and they varied in layout to prevent confusion, one with another, though the symbols themselves were similar.

They were in general use from about 1300 to 1600, often hereditary, and they were used by every trader of standing. Where several branches of the same family were engaged in trading, the same Mark was used but with a slight variation to prevent mistakes.

It is interesting to note that the merchants, who were great benefactors of the churches, had their Marks placed in the church windows. Where they had grants of arms, the arms and the mark were impaled in the same escutcheon.

In 'Piers Plowman's Creed' the following may be found:

'Wyde wyndowes y-wrought,
Y-wryten ful thikke,
Shynen with shapen sheldes,
To shewen aboute,
With merkes of merchauntes
Y-medeled betwene.
Mo than twentie and two
Twyse ynoumbbred.'

Though the Marks are not trade signs in the accepted sense they present an interesting field of study of a closely allied subject and a small selection of them may be found on page 11.

II

BARBERS AND CHEMISTS

Apothecaries, Astrologers, Barbers, Barber-Surgeons, Baths and Shampooers, Chemists, Comb Makers, Corn Cutters, Fortune Tellers, Hairdressers, Hair Sellers, Dentists, Patent Medicine Sellers, Perfumers, Peruke Makers, Quacks, Sweet Powdermen, Tirewomen, Wig Makers

THE Pole of the Barber must surely rank as the most well known of all the signs, surviving when other signs have vanished and still in constant use today.

Modern versions of it appear as striped fluorescent tubes, miniature poles some twelve inches high, and striped electric lamps, but here and there the full-sized pole may be found. The signs today are generally red, white and blue, but the original poles were painted red. The early Barber was a Surgeon as well and when the pole was hanging outside it had a gallipot or a bleeding-dish hanging at the end.

Ancient manuscripts show the pole in use by the Barber with the patient grasping it firmly while the blood-letting was in progress, and as the pole was liable to be spattered with blood, it was painted red. The twisting of white linen bandages around it when not in use gave rise to the striped pole of the present time.

Brass notched soap basins as well as pewter or brass bleeding-dishes were hung on the end of the pole, and the following doggerel, quoted by Larwood and Hotten, is most descriptive:

'His pole with pewter basons hung,
Black, rotten teeth in order strung,
Rang'd cups that in the window stood,
Lined with red rags to look like blood,
Did well his threefold trade explain,
Who shaved, drew teeth and breathed a vein.'

It appears that at one period, the barbers whose activities were confined to hairdressing used a blue and white pole as a sign and no basin was hung at the end. This probably accounts for the red, white and blue of the present, which is a combination of both types of pole, aided no doubt by the fact that they are the national colours. The brass or gilt knob or acorn at the end of the modern pole symbolises the soap basin or the bleeding-dish.

The Barber-Surgeons came into their own after the Edict of the Council of Tours under Pope Alexander III in 1163, which considered that the shedding of blood was incompatible with the holy office of the Clergy. This meant that the Clergy were to confine themselves to the healing art of medicine and that the Barbers were to be the only Surgeons.

At quite an early date Barbers were compelled to dispose of the blood rather than put it on show in the window, which originated the custom of lining the basins with red rags. 'Let no barber be so bold or so daring as to put blood in their windows openly or in view of folks; but let them have it carried privily unto the Thames, under pain of paying two shillings unto the Sheriffs.'

Richard Le Barber was the first Master of the Barbers' Company in London in 1308 and they received their first charter from Edward IV in 1462. The arms of the Barber-Surgeons of London are blazoned:

> 'Quarterly, first and fourth sable, a chevron between three fleams argent, second and third, per pale argent and vert, a spatula in pale azure surmounted of a rose gules charged with another of the first; the first rose regally crowned proper, between the four quarters of a cross of St. George gules charged with a lion passant guardant or.'

The crest is 'an opinicus with wings indorsed or' and the supporters are two lynxes.

The fleams which appear as charges are the knives used for blood-letting. Chambers' Dictionary of 1742 has the entry 'Fleam—a small instrument of pure steel, composed of two or three moveable lancets for bleeding a horse or the like.'

We also read there that:

> 'In England there are two distinct companies of Surgeons now occupying the science or faculty of surgery; the one company called Barbers, the other called Surgeons, which latter are not incorporated. The two are united to sue and be sued by the name of the Masters or Governors and Commonalty of the Mystery of Barbers and Surgeons of London. No person using any Barbery, or shaving, in London, shall occupy any Surgery, letting of blood, or other matter: drawing of teeth only excepted—and no person using the mystery or craft of Surgery shall occupy or exercise the seal or craft of Barbery, or shaving, neither by himself, nor any other for his use. 32 Hen. VIII C42. By the same statute Surgeons are obliged to have signs at their doors.'

In 1745 the Surgeons broke away from the Barbers and were constituted as a separate Company by Act of Parliament. The Barbers retained the Old Hall and its treasures and in 1800 the Surgeons' Company was dissolved and re-formed as the Royal College of Surgeons in London.

Writing in the *Sussex County Magazine* Miss Candlin records two interesting signs of nineteenth-century Barbers, the first in Brighton. This depicted a negro shooting an antelope. The barber claimed to be the inventor of the Antelope Oil which was reputed to be so powerful that if a little were spilled on the pavement, hair would grow on it within twenty-four hours.

The second sign was of a barber named Cooley in High Street, Lewes, which showed Absalom hanging by his long hair from a tree, while his ass was galloping away. Below the picture was written the following doggerel:

> 'Oh, Absalom, unlucky prig,
> Hast thou but worn a periwig,
> For had thy luckless head been shaved,
> Thy life most surely had been saved.'

The name of the Barber below was spelled out in combs, brushes and razors. On the token of Richard White of Canterbury in 1656 the emblem of a Comb was used to indicate his trade.

The Peruke Makers, Wig Makers and Hairdressers used either Locks of Hair or Black, Blue, or Blue and White Perukes as symbols of their trade in much the same way as the modern hairdressing salons display specimen hair styles on models. Blue was the favourite colour and the sign of the Blue Peruke was extremely common.

Some of the letters of Voltaire, written to Swift, are dated from the White Peruke in Maiden Lane. These Perukes were quite expensive and were the target for thieves. Gay wrote in his *Trivia*, Book III:

> 'Nor is thy flaxen wig with safety worn;
> High on the shoulder in a basket borne
> Lurks the sly boy; whose hand to rapine bred,
> Plucks off the curling honours of thy head.'

The Locks of Hair, or the Hand and Lock of Hair were both used as signs by Hair Sellers, though in many cases they were Hairdressers as well.

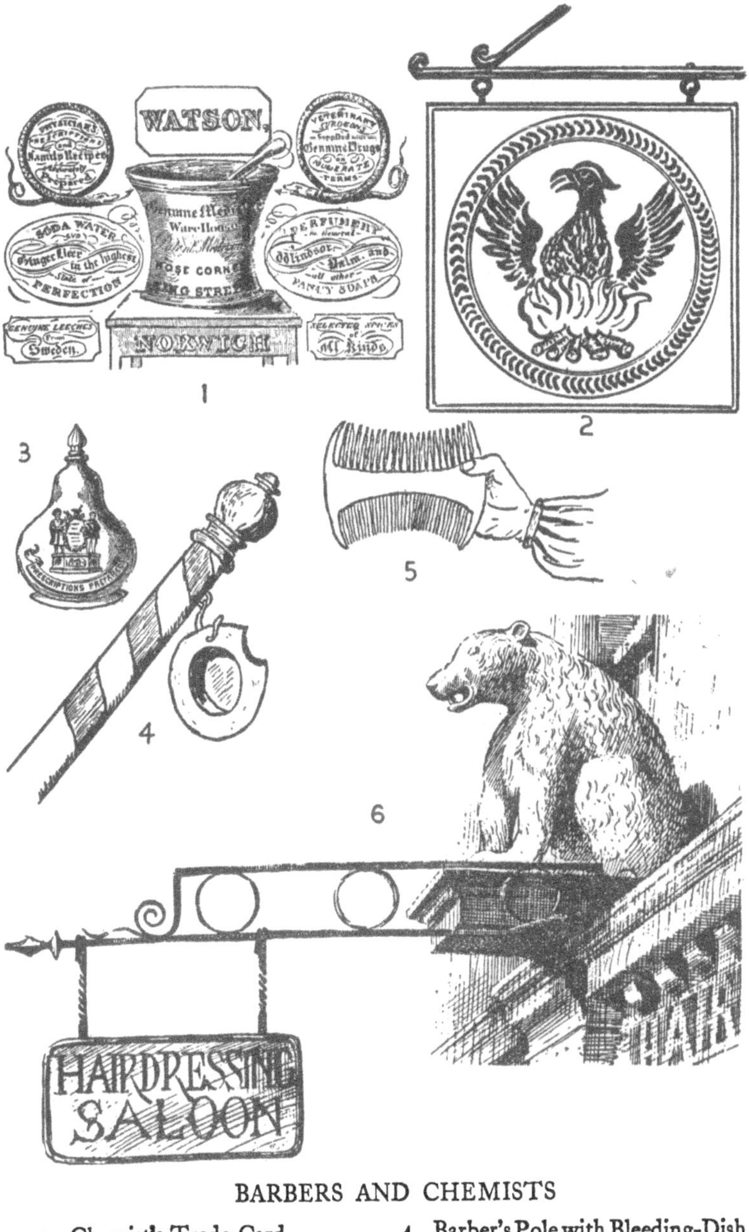

BARBERS AND CHEMISTS

1. Chemist's Trade Card.
2. The Phoenix.
3. Chemist's Phial
4. Barber's Pole with Bleeding-Dish.
5. The Hand and Comb.
6. Gold Bear of Edinburgh (after Fothergill)

The arms of the Comb-makers' Company provided the Comb-makers with their signs which were the Hand and Comb, the Elephant and Comb and the Three Combs. The arms of the Company are blazoned: 'Azure, a lion passant guardant between three combs, or' and the crest is an Elephant standing against a tree. Far back in Roman times the Tirewoman used the sign of the Looking-Glass and Comb, and this device has been found on Roman tombstones.

The Corn Cutters had their own sign, which was quite expressive. It depicted a boy plucking a thorn out of his foot, was called the Boy and Thorn and was associated with foot treatment for centuries.

The Dentists of the eighteenth century, where they were specialists and not Barbers, displayed the sign of the Two Heads, one head showing a perfect set of teeth and the other gapped and broken. In the *London Evening Post* of 1760 there are several advertisements of a dentist in Coventry Street at the sign of the Two Heads. These advertisements are in flowery language and, by our present standards, rather gruesome.

The Baths and Shampooers used the sign of the Turk's Head symbolising the steam baths introduced from the East and known as Turkish Baths. An example of this was the Turk's Head of Alice Neale in James Street, London, about 1730.

The sign of the Civet Cat and the sign of the City of Seville indicated the trade of a Perfumer. The Civet Cat was a natural choice, for this animal provided the civet so widely used in the preparation of perfume and it gave the trade a distinctive sign. In *Chambers' Dictionary* of 1742 we read:

> 'Perfumes were anciently much in use; particularly those wherein musk, ambergreese, and civet enter; they are now generally disused, since people have become sensible of the harm they do the head. In Spain and Italy they are still *à la mode.*'

In Lombard Street in 1705 we find Edward Martin, Sweet Powderman, trading at the Three Herrings and Civet Cat, an odd combination, for only the latter part of the sign can surely represent his trade.

An interesting sign is the Three Arquebusade Bottles of Lewis and David Bourgeois of the Haymarket in 1777, taken from the name of a popular perfume of the period.

The Astrologers adopted the Ball, normally painted black, as their sign, and this was possibly taken from the crystal ball of the Fortune Tellers. Another device used by them was the Head of Lilly, a famous quack, and the Ball and Lilly Head was a common combination. An example in London was the seventeenth-century sign of Thomas Saffold.

The Patent-Medicine Sellers who were barely distinguishable from Quacks used the sign of the Lilly Head as well, their advertisements claiming impossible and magical cures for every ailment then known to man.

The Quacks often used a pointing hand in their signs, and in the early part of the eighteenth century in London the Hand and Ear of S. Ketelby of Exeter Street and the Hand and Face in Blackfriars were well known establishments.

Such signs as the Parrot, the Five Clogs, and the Red M and Dagger were all displayed by Quacks. A favourite was the Anodyne Necklace, and the following advertisement taken from a newspaper of 1718 illustrates the origin of this:

> 'The Anodyne Necklace for children's teeth, women in labour, and distempers of the head: price 5 shillings. Recommended by Dr. Chamberlain. Sold up one pair of stairs at the sign of the Anodyne Necklace, without Temple Bar.'

The Apothecaries and Chemists, from earliest times, have played a major part in the trading pattern of the community, and as such used a wide variety of signs and emblems. One of these, the Pestle and Mortar, is still quite common throughout the country, some indeed are of comparatively modern origin. In some instances, as at Kendal or Edinburgh, the sign is a complete Pestle and Mortar, gilt in the traditional manner, whereas in Norwich a specimen mounted flush with the wall is a half section. The Pestle and Mortar was a natural choice, the most essential piece of equipment in the pounding of drugs, and was a device which could be recognised by the most simple of peasants.

This device was often used on the tokens, as for example by William Dent, Apothecary of Durham, in 1666.

Many Apothecaries, on their tokens, used the arms of the Apothecaries' Company, the blazon of which runs: 'Azure, Apollo proper, a bow in left hand and an arrow in the right or, supplanting a serpent argent.' From these arms Apollo was taken as a sign, and the serpent is regarded as the universal symbol for life and health.

From the brazen Serpent of Moses, from the uplifted Serpent of Egypt, to the present day use of the symbol in the badge of the Royal Army Medical Corps, its meaning has been constant in regard to life, health and even immortality, though it had the alternative symbolisation of the spirit of evil.

The Dragon, ever the symbol of the magical or mysterious, was widely used by the Apothecaries, not only as a sign but as a trade mark, and it was to be found on many of the pots and vessels of the craft. Bel and the Dragon was another version, taken directly from the Apocrypha, though in course of time on some signboards it had been mistakenly represented as a Bell and Dragon. The Dragon could be a link with the Serpent for the word was not exclusive in meaning the fire-breathing monster of our fables and nursery rhymes.

The Salamander, another creature endowed with magical properties, was used as a trade sign by Alchemists

BARBERS AND CHEMISTS

1. Chemist's Phial.
2. Heraldic Fleam (Barbers).
3. Chemist's Trade Card.
4. Pestle and Mortar.
5. Modern Barber's Sign (revolving).
6. The Civet Cat.
7. The Blue Peruke.

and Apothecaries and by its very indestructibility appealed to them. Salamanders appear as supporters to the arms of the Worshipful Company of Ironmongers though there is no record of the beast itself being used as a sign by that trade. The ancient description of them in the *Workes of Armourie* is worth noting:

'Among all the venomenous beastes he is the mightiest of poyson and venome. For if he creepe upon a tree, he infecteth all the apples or other fruit that groweth thereon with his poyson, and killeth them which eate thereof. Which apples, also, if they happen to falle into any pitte of water, the strength of the poyson killeth them that drinkke thereof.'

A seventeenth-century Apothecary in Nottingham called Steven Garner traded at the sign of the Rhinoceros, because it was the crest of the Apothecaries' Company. William Rowe of Newport, Cornwall, about 1666 had a Beehive for his sign, and this is an example of the heraldic origin of some trade emblems, for the Beehive was taken from the arms of his family.

Both Galen and Glauber appeared on the signs of the Apothecaries, mainly the head, that is to say they were advertised as Galen's Head and Glauber's Head. Galen was the Greek physician, born at Pergamus in A.D. 130, who achieved great fame by his many treatises. He is given the credit by some for being the first to establish the consultation of the pulse in diagnosis and prognosis. His authority lasted until well into the sixteenth century and accounts for the choice of his head as a sign.

Glauber was born in Germany in 1604, and was noted for his discovery of Sulphate of Soda or Glauber's Salt, and, being a popular figure, his head was to be found on signboards both in Britain and the Continent.

The Unicorn, which was a favourite sign of the Goldsmiths, was also used by the Apothecaries, for it is a supporter to the Apothecaries' Arms. The horn of this fabulous animal was credited with possessing magical curative properties and the records of the Middle Ages are full of mention of these horns and of their prodigious value.

Similarly the Phoenix, rising again from its ashes, was also widely used as a sign and a fine gilded and carved specimen remained over the door of a chemist called Watson in King Street, Norwich, until a few years ago. The Phoenix often appeared on the drug pots and vessels in the early days, in the same manner as the Dragon.

Both the Buckthorn Tree and Paracelsus appeared on signboards. He was a Swiss savant who died in 1541. After extensive travels in Europe, Paracelsus accepted the chair of medicine at Basle in 1526, had several valuable discoveries to his credit and is sometimes regarded as the founder of modern therapeutics.

Many Chemists' signs were fitted with red and green lighted panels to attract attention and those elegant glass bottles of huge proportions, filled with coloured liquids, may still be found in the older shops. It is no uncommon thing in the provinces to find a chemist's sign today either in the shape of one of these bottles or incorporating them in the general design. Even when the bottles themselves are used, they act as a sign, for they are to be found either in the window or on a high shelf where they are visible from outside. As the Grocer displayed his canister, so the Chemist displayed one or more of those huge jars, generally gold-topped, which bore mysterious names in Latin, accompanied with an heraldic design. These jars, rarer today than a century ago, though not signs in the true sense of the word, nevertheless contributed to the general atmosphere of the Apothecary, helping to give the customer a feeling of confidence in the soundness of the medicines which were sold.

III

FOOD AND DRINK

Bakers, Butchers, Cheesemongers, Confectioners, Coffee Sellers, Cooks, Dairymen, Fishmongers, Fruiterers, Grocers, Mealmen, Millers, Poulterers, Salters, Teamen

THE sign of the Sugarloaf was the most widely used of all the Grocers' signs and was generally arranged in a group of three, in the same manner as the Balls of the Pawnbroker. The Sugarloaf was a conical object and represented the form in which sugar was marketed until the early part of the last century. It resembled a deep conical lampshade and several signs are known to have been converted to take electric lamps when this form of lighting was becoming popular.

In Norwich, when a certain firm of wine merchants and grocers converted their Sugarloaf to an electric sign, the local newspapers commented on 'the transformation from sweetness to light'. The popularity of the Sugarloaf led to its combination with other devices. Examples are the Sugarloaf and Clove of John Betes of Brentwood (1669), the Boar and Sugarloaf of John Clarke of Moorgate (1666), the Plough and Sugarloaf of Robert Smith of Aldersgate Street (1773), the Blackboy and Sugarloaf of Samuel Stone in Leadenhall Street (1754) and the

Sugarloaf and Two Cloves of Edward Woodyard of Norwich (1656).

The use of the Clove on the signboards is taken from the arms of the Worshipful Company of Grocers which are blazoned thus: 'Argent, a chevron gules, between nine cloves sable, three, three and three.' These arms were widely used by traders on their tokens and are possibly the most common of all, due no doubt to the vast quantity of tokens circulated by the Grocers. The crest of the Company is a Camel, which though very little used by the Grocers was adopted by the Confectioners; Anthony Mingay, Grocer of Norwich in 1666, had the sign of the Camel on his token.

As with the single Sugarloaf, the sign of the Three Sugarloaves had to be combined with other devices for the purpose of providing nearby businesses with distinctive signboards. George Farr in Wood Street, London, had the Beehive and Three Sugarloaves (1753), William Scott in Whitechapel traded at the Three Sugarloaves and Crown (1763), John Colcraft in Bishopsgate at the Cannister and Three Sugarloaves (1760), while Ray and Lumley of Cruched Fryers in 1750 traded at the Tea Tub, Three Sugarloaves and Crown. An interesting example is the Three Sugarloaves and Crown of Thomas Rawlinson in Fenchurch Street in 1740, becoming Rawlinson and Davison, and finally Davison, Newman and Company, who still trade at the Three Sugar Loaves and Crown though in Creechurch Lane instead of Fenchurch Street.

There was a sign of the Sugarloaf in Lombard Street before the Great Fire of 1666, and uncommonly enough the local inn at Sible Hedingham in Essex is named the Three Sugarloaves, and has a sign in the traditional manner of the Grocer.

The use of Two Sugarloaves was most uncommon and Joseph Holled of Newgate (about 1665) at the

Two Sugarloaves and Tea-chest is one of the few examples.

The Canister or Golden Cannister was another popular sign amongst the Grocers and Teamen, some of whom were Teamen only, and the Canister generally bore the words, Fine Teas, Fine Green Teas or Green Teas. In most cases the Canister was square though circular ones have been known. Combinations were quite common such as the Crown and Canister of Joseph Lloyd in Chandos Street (1760) and the Tea Chest and Canister of William Sandys in Fleet Street (1760), and the honours were evenly divided between Golden Cannisters and Green Cannisters, the spelling also varying between one N and two. The Tea Tub and the Tea Chest were the main signs of the Teamen and an eighteenth-century Tea Dealer in London had the original sign of the Walking Leaf. This was taken from an East Indian insect of that name with a somewhat unusual appearance.

The following lines by John Tatham (1659) about the wares of the Grocer give some idea of the importance of the selling of spices:

> 'Heart-pleasing Cinnamon, Cloves, Mace, Nutmegs, are
> From famed Arabia brought,
> Then Senna, Rhubarb, China roots that do
> Not only purify but strengthen too,
> Sarsaparilla. . . .'

The Fig and the Lemon Tree were both used as signs, and in eighteenth-century Edinburgh Andrew Douglas in Marlins Wynd sold tea, sugar, coffee, rum and brandy at the sign of the Crown and Lemon Tree, while George Snowball in the Strand, London, traded at the Figg Tree.

Amongst the unusual tea signs in London we find the West India Planter of James Spalding, Whitechapel (1755), the Chinese Porter of John Showrd in Cockspur

Street (1760) and the China Man and Tea Tree of John Harling in the Strand (1764).

The Grasshopper is surely one of the most interesting of the signs of the Grocers, for at first glance its connection with their trade is not apparent. The use of the Grasshopper dates from the time of Sir Thomas Gresham, that eminent Elizabethan merchant who founded the Royal Exchange and whose crest and sign it was. In Pennant's *Account of London*, 1813, the following may be found:

> 'The shop of the great Sir Thomas Gresham stood in Lombard Street: it is now occupied by Messrs Martin, bankers, who are still in possession of the original sign of that illustrious person—the Grasshopper. Were it mine, that honourable memorial of so great a predecessor should certainly be placed in the most ostentatious situation I could find.'

The Grasshopper as a device is said to bring good luck and the site of the Merchant's house was 68, Lombard Street, opposite Abchurch Lane. The use of the sign spread from London to the provinces where it was widely used, and as late as 1795 a new Grasshopper was installed over the shop of Nathaniel Roe, Grocer, London Street, Norwich. In London in 1760 a Grocer named Sedgwick traded as the Original Grasshopper in Bishopsgate. Isaac Thornton in Fleet Street had the Grasshopper and Tea Cannister (1750), and William Thorns in White Cross Street displayed the Grasshopper in 1770.

A sign which could well be our national emblem, the Teapot, was used by many nineteenth-century Grocers, and a few of these signs still remain. They were made of wood, held at least a couple of gallons, and were gilded. A fine specimen may be seen in the Strangers' Hall Museum, Norwich. It dates from the middle of the last century and was known as the Golden Teapot.

As a subsidiary sign some Teamen had a life-sized figure of a Chinaman, correctly garbed, which stood in

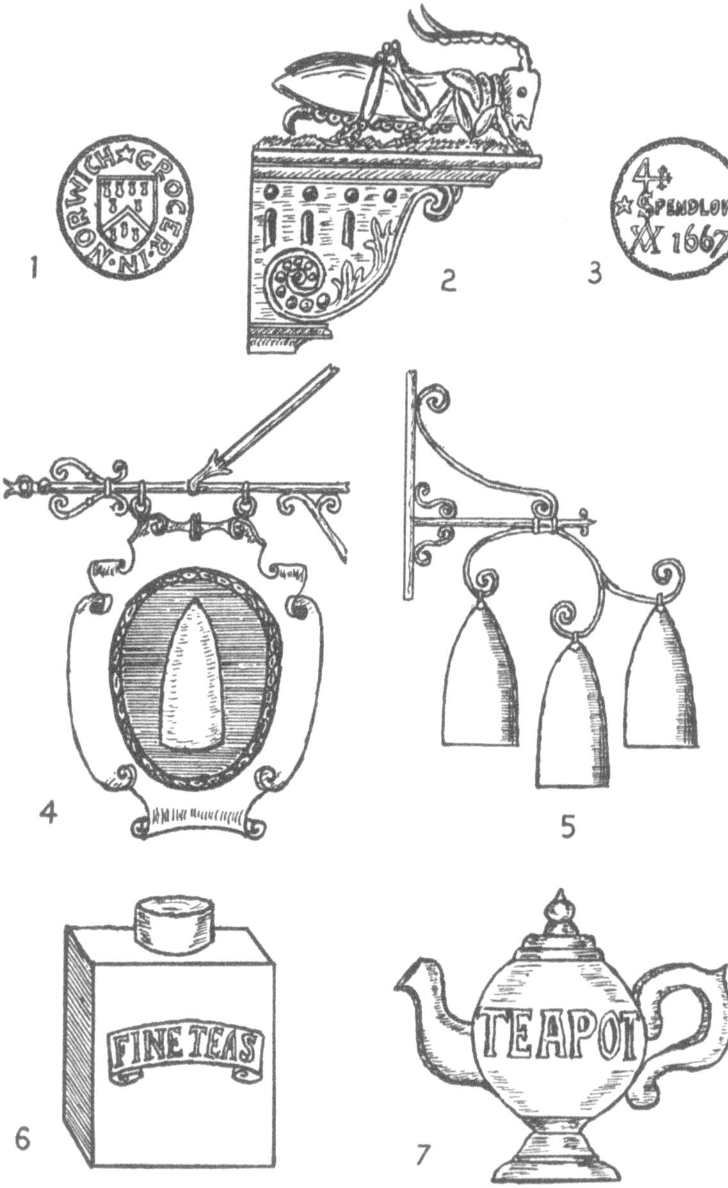

FOOD AND DRINK

1. Grocer's Token, obverse, showing Grocers' arms.
2. Grasshopper of Lombard St.
3. Grocer's Token showing his mark.
4. Sugarloaf Sign.
5. Sign of the Three Sugarloaves.
6. Golden Canister.
7. Golden Teapot of R. H. Fox, Norwich.

the doorway or just inside the shop, and held a tray of samples. Similarly Moorish figures served the same purpose with the Coffee Sellers, and some shops had both figures, side by side. The sign of the Coffee Mill was also used, for instance the famous London example of Pickering and Clarke in St James (1760), later Joseph Browne (1793), and finally Berry Brothers (1801), who were wine merchants but kept the Coffee Mill sign. The shop still retains this ancient sign.

The use of the letter Z as a sign of the grocery trade is recorded, possibly standing for Zinzibar (ginger) or a corruption of the figure 4. The figure 4 was used in Scotland as a Grocers' sign and though its origin is unknown it may have meant that their wares came from the four quarters of the globe.

The Grocers also used various signs not belonging to their trade, such as the Bunch of Grapes of Thomas Gasley of Little Britain (1666), the Boar's Head and Three Arrows of Nat Child in the Strand (1667), the Saracen's Head in Westminster (1666), the Blackboy of Edward Crayford of Canterbury (1664), and the Blackmoor's Head of Hugh James in Fleet Street (1764).

The two principal signs of the Cheesemongers were the Dairy Maid and Churn (John Whithorne, St. Catherines, 1666) and the Dairy Maid and Cheese (Thomas Miller, Wapping, about 1750). Richard Barrett of St James's (1665) had a Cheese Taster on his token, Thomas Newbery of Creed Lane had a Cheese Knife (1669) and Thomas Baker of Canterbury used the sign of the Hand and Scales (1667). Two London Cheesemongers traded at the sign of the Dolphin and B. Norman of Snow Hill in 1667 used the Naked Boy, neither of which can be regarded as in general use by the cheese trade.

The Confectioners, whose wares had many links with the East, chose the Camel and the Pineapple as their two main signs. The Camel was taken from the crest of the Grocers' Company and the Pineapple for its flavour because it was widely used in confectionery.

Anthony Golston, Confectioner in the Strand, had the sign of the Four Cloves (1667), Will Bryan of Cambridge the Three Cloves (1652), L. Goodwy of Norwich had the Camel (1666) and William Weedon of Fleet Street traded at the Golden Pheasant (1760). A rather unusual sign for a Confectioner was the Frying Pan and Three Garbs of Edward Farmer of Southwark (1669). Garbs presumably came from the arms of the Company of Bakers but the Frying Pan has no link.

The arms of the Worshipful Company of Bakers are blazoned thus: 'Gules, a balance between three garbs or, on a chief barry wavy of four argent and azure an arm embowed proper vested gules, cuffed or, issuing from clouds affixed to the upper part of the centre of the chief, of the fifth, radiated of the last, between two anchors of the second, the hand supporting the balances.'

The two most common signs of the Bakers (the Hand and Scales and the Wheatsheaf or the Three Wheatsheaves) were taken from these arms, as we see in such examples as Thomas Humpheris of Cheltenham at the Three Birds and Wheatsheaf (1669); Abraham Ansell of Bocking at the Wheatsheaf and Scales (about 1668); and John Sharpe, Mealman, of Golden Lane, London, at the Three Wheatsheaves (1666).

Their tokens show other devices such as the Pie Crust of Robert Millard of Caxton (1668), the Nine Bread Rolls of Thomas Hunt in the Strand (1666), the Windmill of Will Smaley, Without Bishopsgate (about 1666) and the Baker's Peel of Thomas Payne of Bury St Edmunds (1668).

The Mealmen, close associates of the Bakers, used similar signs, mainly incorporating the Wheatsheaf, and from their tokens we find devices of the Wheatsheaf and

Three Birds of Nicholas Hawett in Holborn (about 1666), the Windmill and Packhorse of John Pearson in White Hart Yard (about 1666), the Pelican of John Browne in Soho (1664) and the Three Arrows of Thomas Skelton in Shire Lane (about 1666). Daniel Hurst of Hitchen, Oatmeal Maker in 1666, had the sign of the Man and Sieve, Henry Edwards, Cornchandler in Holborn, traded at the Dog (1668) and Richard Shepheard, Cornchandler in High Holborn, displayed the Three Horseshoes (1666).

The Millers had no need of signs, the mill itself indicated their trade, but on their tokens the devices were always associated with the mill itself. Jonathan Kingham of Woburn Mill, Beds., showed the Mill Rind and Wheel (about 1666) and Thomas Bye of Reading had the Mill Cramp and Sack (about 1666). Both the Dusty Miller and the Millstone appear as inn signs, but there is no record of the former being used by Millers, though the latter is a possibility.

The Fruiterers had one traditional sign in the Lemon Tree; three examples were known in Covent Garden alone. The arms of the Fruiterers' Company were also used and these are blazoned: 'Azure, on a mount in base vert, the tree of paradise, environed with the serpent between Adam and Eve all proper.' It is worth noting that the sign of the Orange Tree, which one would expect to be used by the Fruiterers as well as the Lemon Tree, was not used by them at all, though the device does appear on the signboards of the Italian Warehousemen.

The source of milk was a natural choice for the sign of a Dairyman, in Roman times a Goat and in a later age the Cow. Life-size models of Dairy Cows were quite common in the nineteenth century and these were generally mounted on a plinth above the shop. Norwich used to have a fine specimen, which at the time of the visit of King Edward VII was taken in procession on a cart

FOOD AND DRINK

1. Modern Sign of the Herring Industry Board.
2. Roman Signs: Goat, Dairy. Mill, Baker.
3. The Haunch of Venison.
4. Fishmongers' Arms.
5. Butchers' Arms.
6. Whistling Oyster.
7. Teamen's Canister.
8. Bakers' Wheatsheaf.
9. Confectioners' Pineapple.
10. Grocers' Coffee Mill.

around the city as part of a series of tradesmen's tableaux. This sign was made of wood and painted to resemble a Jersey Cow, and it is unfortunate that it was destroyed when the dairy closed down.

Few signs are recorded amongst the Butchers. Perhaps the well-stocked shops of our ancestors made their use unnecessary, but Elijah's Raven was used by one London butcher who showed the bird with a chop in its mouth. In Victorian times the butchers' shops frequently had a pair of Golden Ox Heads above the window, one each side of the owner's name. In many cases the shops were fitted out with glazed tiles in various colours, and below the window or in the doorway a fine specimen of beef on the hoof formed the principal part of the design. In the case of the Pork Butchers, the Pig was naturally used and though these are not signboards they can surely rank as signs of the Butchery Trade.

The use of the Bulls' Heads comes from the arms of the Company of Butchers, which are blazoned thus: 'Azure, two slaughter axes indorsed in saltire argent handled or, between three bulls' heads, couped of the second, armed of the third, viz. two in fesse and one in base; on a chief argent a boar's head coupled gules between two block-brushes (i.e. bunches of knee holly) vert.'

The crossed Slaughter Axes were also used as a sign, and on a token issued by John Baker in 1669 this device appears. The Provision Sellers used the sign of the Ham and Tongues. Heal records an Oilman in the Strand at the sign of the Ham in 1766, while Matthew Dyne, Bacon Seller of Butcher Row, Temple Bar, traded at the Side of Bacon in 1666.

The Poulterers, very important traders in the hey-day of signboards, generally used the sign of the Swan. The Swan was one of the principal items on the menu at the civic feasts, and its use on the signboards of inns is widespread even today. It was taken from the arms of the Company of Poulterers which are blazoned: 'Argent, on a chevron between three storks as many swans proper,' the supporters being two pelicans.

James Haydye, Poulterer, Without Cripplegate, in 1666 had the sign of the Three Storks, Richard Underwood of Holborn had the Running Hare (about 1666), and John Dollen, Poulterer, near the Maypole, Strand, had the Bell and Maypole.

The arms of the Cooks' Company were used on their tokens and are blazoned: 'Argent, a chevron engrailed gules between three columbines proper stalked and leaved vert.' The crest is a cock pheasant and the supporters are a buck and a hind. The Cooks were anciently known as the Pastelers or Pie Bakers but there is very little evidence of the general use of signs by them. The token of Henry Mattershaw of Salisbury about 1666 shows a Cook's Knife, Robert Morley of Fleet Street had the sign of the Golden Pheasant (1765) and Richard Perry of Oxford Street had the Pheasant (1800), both the latter being taken from the crest of the Company.

The Salters, who dealt not only in salt and salted foods, but in flax, hemp, logwood, cochineal, potashes, etc., used the arms of the Company of Salters as a sign. These are blazoned: 'Per chevron azure and gules, three covered salts or sprinkling salts argent' and the supporters are two otters.

There is little information about other signs which may have been used. Richard Norwood of Hosier Lane had the Horse's Head (1668) and John Sheldon of Coleman Street had the Three Crowns (1668), but neither of these signs was peculiar to Salters. The token of John Dickens of Backwell (1669) had the crest of the Salters' Company, an arm holding a covered salt sprinkler, and that of Bridget Wooley in the Barbican (about 1666) the three salts and chevron from the arms.

The signs of the Fishmongers, though varied, indicated a wide use of the arms of the Fishmongers' Company, a custom which has remained even to this day. These arms are blazoned: 'Azure, three dolphins naiant in pale argent finned and ducally crowned or, between two pair of lucies in saltire (the sinister surmounting the dexter) proper, over the nose of each lucy a ducal crown of the third: on a chief gules three pair of keys, endorsed in saltire or.' The supporters are a merman and a mermaid, both of which have appeared on the trade tokens. William Robinson of Henley-on-Thames (1668) used the Dolphin on his token and Nicholas Orum of Oxford (1657) had the sign of the Lobster. It is interesting to note that the Herring Industry Board uses the device of a Crowned Herring, clad in a cloak of ermine, in all its advertisements and that this symbol appears on the windows of fishmongers throughout the land.

Larwood and Hotten record the Postboy as a fishmonger's sign at Sherbourne Lane, London, where in 1759 green native oysters were sold at 3/3 a barrel. Both the Whistling Oyster and the Oyster Girl were used by London Fishmongers, the latter at 13, Charles Street, Soho, in 1790. In Victorian times the provincial fishmongers frequently used large stuffed fish as signs, and a few of them survive today. The multiple firm of Macfisheries uses a sign which consists of the familiar blue and white saltire of St Andrew and four fish, one in each quarter. This device appears on signs hung outside the shops and on the paper and bags used for wrapping.

IV

TOBACCO AND INTOXICANTS

Brewers, Distillers, Pipe Makers, Snuff Makers, Tobacconists, Vintners

THE most common sign of the Distiller was the Still. This was varied as the Man and Still, the Golden Still, the Plough and Still and the Angel and Still. The Distiller sold quite a range of wares, as we see in this advertisement from the *Norwich Mercury* of March, 1727:

'William Furly is removed from the Door next the Jayl in the Market-place to the Still and Black Boy in the Dove Lane, where he distils and sells Royal-Geneva, Clove-water, Aniseed, Wormwood, Orange, Carraway, and Cholick-water, Usquebaugh, Aqua Mirabilis, Dr Stephen's, Cinnamon, Rosa-solis, Golden-Cordial, and Cardemum: Also all sorts of Brandies, from 2s. 6d. to 8s. per gallon; rectify'd Spirits of Wine, Spirits for Lamps, Hungary-water and Vinegar. . . . N.B. His Wife sells all sorts of Millenary Goods at the same Place.'

The token of Richard Cottam, Distiller, of Reading in 1669 showed the sign of a Still, while many tokens and signboards showed the Juniper Tree. The Juniper Tree was appropriate for a distiller, for from its berries is obtained the oil of juniper used in the manufacture of Gin.

The arms of the Company of Distillers are blazoned thus: 'Azure, a fesse wavy argent, in chief the sun in splendour, encircled with a cloud distilling drops of rain, all proper, in base a distillatory double armed or, on a fire proper with two worms and bolt receivers of the second.' The supporters are a Russian and an Indian (with bow and arrows) and the crest is a sheaf of barley and grapes.

These arms were used by Distillers on their sign-boards; by Edward Jemmitt in the Strand (1750) for instance, at the sign of The Distillers' Arms against the Fountain Tavern.

The Vintners had two common signs, the Bunch of Grapes and the Three Tuns, both of which are still widely used by inns and taverns. The Three Tuns are taken from the Vintners' arms which are blazoned: 'Sable, a chevron between three tuns argent.' The Brewers' arms also have the tuns as a charge and their blazon runs 'Gules, on a chevron argent between three pair of barley garbes in saltire or, three tuns sable, hooped of the third.' Crest 'On a wreath a demi Moorish woman, couped at the knees proper her hair dishevelled or, habited sable frettee argent, her arms extended, holding in each hand three ears of barley of the second.'

An interesting token issued by William Tanner, Brewer of Ely (about 1666) showed the sign of the Sparger. The sparger was a vessel with pierced arms for distributing 'liquor' over malt or grains in the mash tub, by swinging round on a centre pin.

The Innholders belonged to a separate guild and the arms of the Innholders' Company are blazoned 'Azure, a chevron per pale gules and argent counterchanged, between three garbs or, on a chief argent two batons crossed at each sable in saltire, the dexter surmounted by the sinister, commonly called St Julian's cross.' Crest 'An estoile of sixteen points or, issuing from clouds in base proper.' Supporters 'Two horses reguardant argent.'

The Tobacconists, in common with the Snuffmen and the Pipe Makers, had several traditional signs, including the Tobacco Rolls. This sign was widely used and may be found even today hanging in the doorways of old-established Tobacconists. The rolls represented the form in which tobacco was shipped in the early days; they were flat, circular cakes between ten and twelve inches in diameter, strung together with pack thread. The actual signs were made of wood and the rolls were painted black and gold alternately. The token of John Carter of Clophill in 1666 showed a tobacco roll and in the doorway of Chidwick's shop in Cannon Street, Dover, a specimen exists at the present time.

Tradition associates the introduction of tobacco into Britain with Sir Walter Raleigh, and his portrait appeared on many tobacconists' signs.

> 'Great Britain to great Raleigh owes,
> This plant and country where it grows.'

This comes from the *General Advertiser* of March 13, 1784, taken from the tobacco wrapping of a London Tobacconist.

The Pipe Makers generally used the sign of the Three Pipes and the sign of the Golden Pipe in Norwich indicated a Tobacconist's and Ironmonger's business. The business was founded in 1601 and closed in 1914, and by the name of Buckle was mentioned in the diary of Parson Woodforde (1758–1802). The sign was a long-stemmed small bowl pipe, which was made of cast iron and broken up when the business ceased. The combination of Tobacconist and Ironmonger was not uncommon in the provinces in the seventeenth and eighteenth centuries, though in every case the tobacco department was eventually discontinued, leaving only the ironmongery. (The Golden Pipe closed down as Palmer and Sons, Ironmongers.)

The Pipe Makers' Guild (Charter of James I in 1619) had as supporters to their arms 'Two young Moors all

1

6

2

3

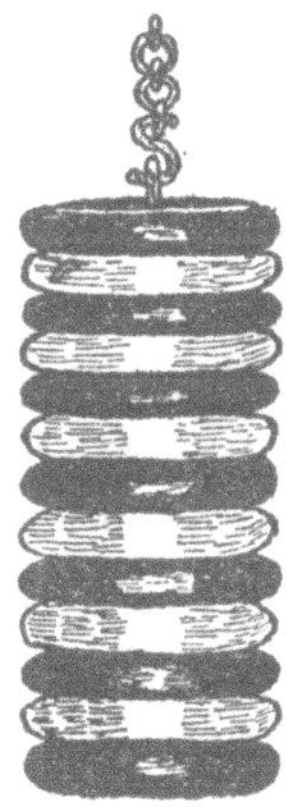

7

4

5

TOBACCONISTS.

1. Sir Roger de Coverley.
2. Black Boy.
3. Tobacconist's Sign.
4. Abel Drugger.
5. Black Boy.
6. Trade Card of David Wishart of the Highlander, Thistle and Crown.
7. Tobacco Rolls in Strangers' Hall Museum, Norwich.

proper, wreathed about the loins with tobacco leaves vert.' The crest was also a Moor 'in his dexter hand a tobacco pipe and in his sinister hand a roll of tobacco, all proper.'

These Moors or Turks as they were usually called were quite common as tobacconists' signs, as well as the Blackamoors and Black Boys who were portrayed as Negroes, and nearly all of them wore a skirt of tobacco leaves.

Fothergill in his *Stones and Curiosities of Edinburgh* records two fine Turks as Tobacconists' signs in 1910. The first was a tall carved wooden figure, turbaned, in long flowing robes and smoking a pipe which came below his knees. Known as the Leith Street Turk, he stood in an alcove at Thomson and Porteous of Leith Street, and as usual with these valuable figures was taken inside every night for safe custody.

The second figure, known as the West Register Street Turk, was much smaller than the first, and smoked a cheroot instead of a pipe. He had a turban which sported a crescent and wore baggy trousers, sash and a loose-fitting coat. This figure was used as a Tobacconist's sign in South Bridge Street, Edinburgh from about 1840 to 1900, but its age is unknown.

The Black Boy, The Virginian, The Virginia Planter, all take us back to the tobacco plantations, and some of the signboards show a still as well; for instance the Angel and Still of Mr Bathurst of Billingsgate (1770) and the Black Boy and Still of Mr Noss of Fleet Street (1750). The Black Boy often appeared as the Black Boy's Head or, as with John Cater of Fleet Street in 1770, the Blackmoor's Head.

Fothergill mentions a Tobacconist's sign in Edinburgh which was known as the Grassmarket Nigger, and which was the head of a negro with a short pipe in his mouth. It came to Grassmarket in 1866 from Richardson of West Bow where it had been from well before 1838 and it is believed to have come from Glasgow in the first place.

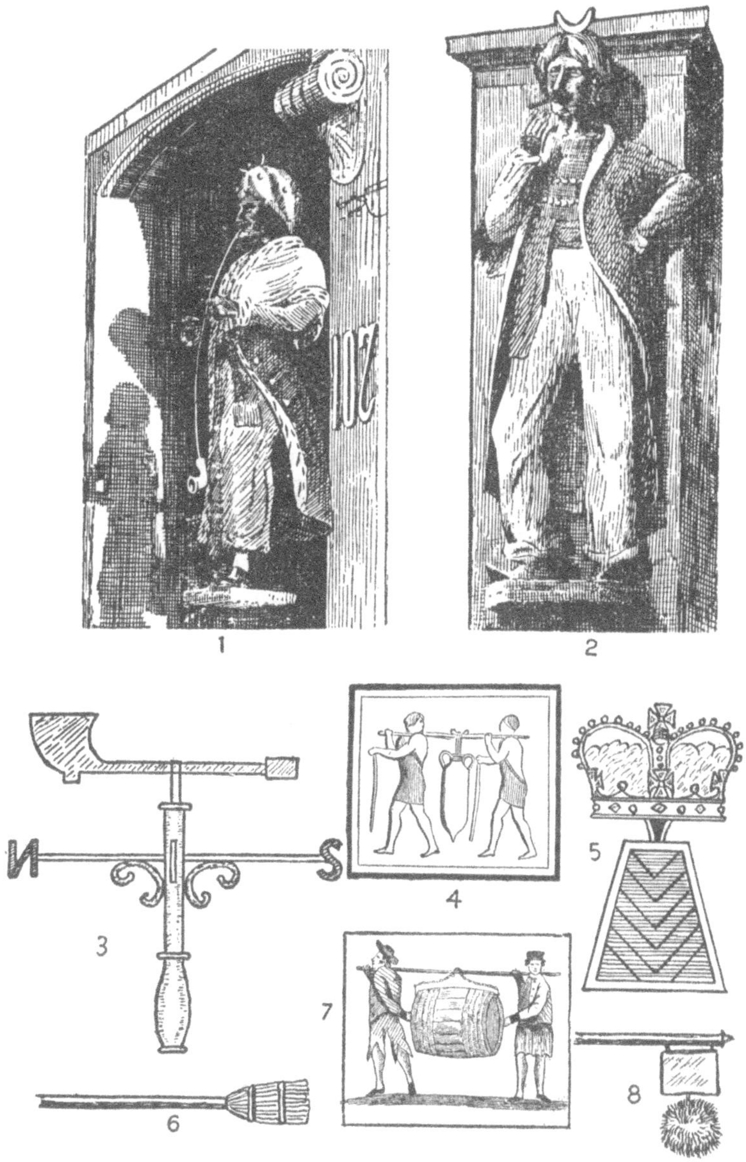

TOBACCO AND INTOXICANTS.

1. Leith Street Turk, Edinburgh.
2. West Register Street Turk, Edinburgh.
3. Pipe Maker's Weathervane.
4. Roman Wine Merchant.
5. Rasp and Crown.
6. Bush of Medieval Wine Shop.
7. Two Jolly Brewers.
8. Bush of Medieval Wine Shop.

The Green Man and Still was another sign of the Tobacconists, the device taken possibly from the Distillers' arms. The Green Man in this case was a mutilation of the Indian who is one of the supporters, and painted green to make a wild man.

The Snuff Men or Snuff Makers used the principal tool of their trade for a sign, the Rasp. These signs normally appeared as the Crown and Rasp or the Rasp and Crown, and it is at the Rasp and Crown that the old-established firm of Fribourg and Treyer in the Haymarket trade today.

Sir Roger de Coverley has been used as a sign in the tobacco trade and Larwood and Hotten suggest that this was due to the essays of the *Spectator*. The Man in the Moon was certainly used on the Tobacconists' papers. The illustration shows a countryman with a tankard in one hand and a pipe in the other with the legend 'Who'll Smoak with Ye Man in Ye Moon' underneath.

The most popular of all the signs of the Tobacconists must surely be the Highlander, generally a carved wooden figure, mostly life-size, and often beautifully painted in the colours of a famous Highland regiment. Though many fine signs have been known in Scotland, not one of them appears to have been made in that country; they were all purchased in England and mostly made in London.

The oldest Highlander sign in Edinburgh, that of John Sinclairs of Leith Street, came originally from Gateshead and the sign shown at the Scottish National Exhibition in 1908 was purchased in a London sale room. The small Black Watch model of Mr Craik of Edinburgh was once stolen (according to Fothergill) by officers of the Black Watch and put up as a sentry on the Castle Rock.

The popularity of the sign is shown by the fact that Charles Dickens in *Little Dorrit* assumed that it was the normal thing for all tobacco shops to possess one. He writes:

'The tobacco business round the corner of Horsemonger Lane was of too modest a character to support a life-size Highlander, but it maintained a little one on a bracket on the door post, who looked like a fallen cherub that had found it necessary to take to a kilt.'

It is believed that the origin of the Highlander for a sign is to be found in its use by David Wishart of Coventry Street in the early part of the eighteenth century. It indicated that he sold Scots Snuff as distinct from Bristol Snuff which was very popular at that time. His sign was the Highlander, Thistle and Crown and became also the sign of a Jacobite rendezvous. Two years after the rebellion of 1745 a bill was passed making Highland garb illegal, and this was not repealed until 1782. During that time our Highlanders outside the tobacco shops must have been the only ones legally wearing the garb, and it is interesting to note that the business of David Wishart who started the fashion is still carried on in Panton Street, the original Coventry Street shop having been pulled down in 1880.

The old trade card of David Wishart, dated 1720, reads:

'David Wishart at ye Highlander, Thistle and Crown at ye upper end of St James's Hay Market, In Coventry Street London Makes & sells all sorts of Snuff (Viz) Prime London Snuff, high & low dry'd Scots Snuff, plain Spanish, old Havana, Rappee, Oronoko, & Herb Snuff, fine & coarse Pigtail, and best Tobacco; Wholesale & Retail at ye lowest Rates.'

A newspaper article which appeared after the bill of 1747 reads:

'We hear that the dapper wooden Highlanders, who guard so heroically the doors of snuff-shops, intend to petition the Legislature, in order that they may be excused from complying with the act of Parliament with regard to their change of dress; alledging that they have ever been faithful subjects to his Majesty, having constantly supplied his Guards with a pinch out of their Mulls when they marched by them, and so far from engaging in any Rebellion, that they have never entertained a rebellious thought; whence they humbly hope that they shall not be put to the Expense of buying new cloaths.'

Millers, Tobacconists of London Street, Norwich, are in the happy position of owning two Highlanders. The smaller remains inside the shop while the life-size specimen stands invitingly in the doorway, both are in perfect condition and their paintwork is lovingly cared for. The Scotsman, as the one in the doorway is known locally, is dressed in the uniform of the Black Watch, that most famous of all Highland Regiments. Its origin dates back to 1725 and it was raised in 1729 and embodied as the forty-third Regiment in 1740, becoming the forty-second in 1749. In common with most of the Highlander signs, these hold a snuff horn or mull in their left hands, indicating their origin as Snuff Makers' signs.

Above the shop of W. H. Chidwick of Cannon Street, Dover, there is a stone figure of a Highlander far above the reach of passers-by, dating from 1890. In the doorway stands a painted wooden Highlander labelled 1840, but it is believed to be much older than this. No record of these figures would be complete without a mention of Phineas, the Highlander of Catesbys, which has been the central figure in many of the frolics of medical students from University College, London.

Included in any list of these Tobacco Highlanders would be the seven-feet-high specimen of Churchmans of Ipswich, the very small figure of Dickens of Cheltenham, the small one in Salisbury Museum, and Bewlays' fine figure which used to adorn the Strand. Another fine specimen in Cheltenham is chained to the wall by his shoulder and the London Museum in Kensington Palace has the largest collection in existence, five Highlanders in all.

Robert Louis Stevenson in the *Dynamiter* gives a detailed picture of the Tobacconist of the period, the Bohemian Cigar Divan, and he writes:

'The entrance was adorned with one of those gigantic Highlanders of wood which have almost risen to the standing of antiquities.'

V

CLOTHING AND ASSOCIATED TRADES

Bodice Makers, Clothworkers, Drapers, Dyers, Feltmakers, Furriers, Framework Knitters, Glovers, Girdlers, Hatters, Hosiers, Lacemen, Linen Drapers, Mercers, Merchant Taylors, Milliners, Needle Makers, Silkmen and Silk Throwers, Skinners, Slop Sellers, Tailors, Weavers, Woolcombers, Woollen Drapers, Woolmen

THE Woolcombers used the principal tool of their trade, the Woolcomb, as their sign, and many examples of this may be found on their trade tokens. In 1666 Mathew Munday of Taunton used this device, and in 1654 Henry Dunscombe of Taunton had a Wool Card on his token. The token of Thomas Sandes of Kendal is worth mentioning, for on the obverse is a Teasel and a Woolhook, and on the reverse a Woolcomb. This token is an early one dating from 1656.

The Woolmen's arms 'Gules, a woolpack argent' are to be found on tokens and were used, for instance, by Joseph Fishpoole of Billericay in 1669. The Woolpack became a favourite choice as an inn sign, and in rural districts today the sign is still common. Fothergill records a fine sign in St Andrew's Square, Edinburgh, which consisted of three large gilded bales of wool, each bale bearing the word WOOL in large letters.

The patron saint of the Woolcombers was Bishop Blaize and his likeness was used as a sign. St Blasius, Bishop of Sebaste in Cappadocia, is depicted holding the iron comb which was used to tear the flesh from his body, and in Kendal there is an inn with a fine modern sign showing the saint. Years ago his patronal day was the occasion for pageantry and festivity in the wool districts, but today only a mere echo of it remains.

The Woollen Drapers had a wide variety of signs, but the most common was the Golden Fleece. This ancient device, recorded as the object of Jason's quest on the voyage of the Argonauts, in signboard lore is sometimes called the Golden Lamb. The Golden Fleece is mentioned in some of the ancient Indian hymns, the fleece being used as a filter for the golden wine. Amongst the Brahmins it was adored, after being saturated with the sacred wine, as embodying the presence of the deity Indra.

Larwood and Hotten mention that the Golden Fleece was used commonly as an inn sign, and they suggest that though it was appropriate for a Draper, it had a double meaning for an inn, implying the traveller might be fleeced within.

The Lamb was popular as a Draper's sign and was often found in such combinations as the Lamb and Star, the Lamb and Seven Stars or the Crown and Lamb.

The use of the Woolpack by the Woollen Drapers was quite common, sometimes accompanied by a Negro Boy, a Naked Boy or a Golden Boy. Another device, that of the Seven Stars, was widely used and this has an interesting origin. The Seven Stars was associated with the early astral creeds and originally the Seven Stars were the Pleiades, the group in the neck of the constellation Taurus. In Greek legends they were the seven daughters of Atlas and the nymph Pleione.

Later, due perhaps to the Phoenician navigators, the Seven Stars came to mean the Ursa Major, the Great Bear or Charles' Wain, and Ursa Minor the Lesser Bear, both constellations consisting of seven. The link with the Woollen Drapers is not apparent, but there is no doubt about their use of this device; for instance the token of John Sparrow of Ipswich in 1659 shows it, and Samuel Leech of Bedford Street in London traded at the Seven Stars and King's Arms in 1752.

The sellers of wool had the sign of the Spinning Wheel, and in Frederick Street, Edinburgh, a fine Golden Spinning Wheel may still be seen above the door of a wool shop.

Many of the Drapers' tokens bore the Drapers' Arms and these were blazoned: 'Azure, three clouds proper, radiated in base or, each surmounted with a triple crown or.' Other tokens of Drapers include the Wounded Hart of Henry Theobald of Pulham Market, the Fleur de Lys and Crown of James Warwell of Boxford and the Man in The Moon of Will Robinson of Norwich in 1667.

The Linen Drapers had many signs and a popular choice was that of the Three Nuns. As much of the fine embroidery and other similar work came from the religious houses it was an obvious choice and linked up with another one of their signs, the Three Angels. No doubt Angels were chosen because of their traditional portrayal in long, flowing robes, most appropriate for the clothing trade.

The Packhorse and Fustian is an interesting sign, for in the seventeenth and eighteenth centuries it represented the transport of one of the principal items of their stock in trade. Fustian, the name derived from a suburb of Cairo called Fostat from which the stuff first came, was formerly a coarse cloth of flax and linen. Latterly the term was used for a twilled cotton cloth with a short nap and in some cases the sign just showed a single roll of

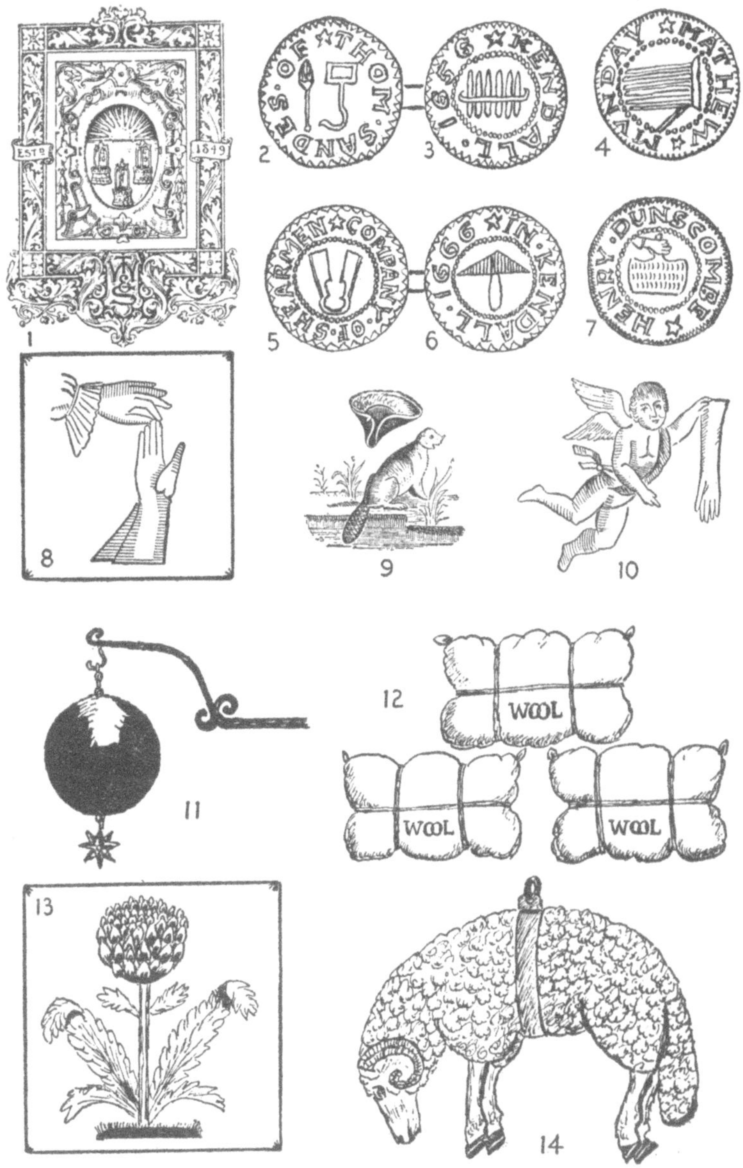

CLOTHING AND ASSOCIATED TRADES (i)

1. Example of Rebus. Three Wells and Sun for T. Wells & Son, Hatters, Norwich.
2. Teasel and Woolhook.
3. Woolcomb.
4. Woolcomb.
5. Croppers.
6. Teasel Brush.
7. Woolcard.
8. Hand and Glove.
9. Hat and Beaver. (after Larwood and Hotton)
10. Angel and Glove. (after Larwood and Hotten)
11. Golden Ball and Star.
12. Three Bales of Wool of Edinburgh.
13. Artichoke.
14. Golden Fleece.

Fustian or perhaps a couple of rolls without the pack-horse.

Amongst the tokens issued by Drapers may be found those of Thomas Juxson of Brecknock in 1669 with the sign of the Shears and Glove, Henry Pitman of Morsley in 1668 with the Shuttle, and John Parrett of Shire Lane, London, 1667 at the Sword and Buckler.

The Wheatsheaf, sign of the Bakers, and appearing on the arms of the Brewers' Company as barley garbs, was often used by the Linen Drapers, but there seems to be no explanation for this choice. Heal records that Thomas Bentley of St Paul's Churchyard (1796), Edward Eyre of York Street (1739), Alexander Scholar of New Bond Street (1785) and several others were all Linen Drapers using the sign of the Wheatsheaf.

Similarly, the Unicorn of the Chemists and Goldsmiths was appropriated by the Linen Drapers; London examples included Thomas West of the Strand (1775), Nathaniel Hall in Parliament Street (1772), and Finney, Sirdefield and Clarke in Newgate Street (1777).

Many of the signs of the Drapers were common to the Mercers, the Hen and Chickens and the Blackmoor's Head being two notable examples. Both these signs were widely used by Linen Drapers and must be regarded as essential in any list. An interesting sign displayed by a London Draper in 1750 was that of Jeremiah Hemsworth in White Horse Yard, Drury Lane, who traded at the sign of the Two Fustian Rolls, Rose and Crown, typical of the combination signs of the period.

The Weavers' traditional sign was the Spinning Wheel and Joseph Webb, a Flaxman of Leadenhall Street, in 1668 used this device. Abraham Derrix of Norwich, Weaver, in 1665 had the sign of The Fleece and the token of Thomas Dan of Wye in 1652 shows a Coiled Snake. Heal records that Francis Rybot, Weaver, of Raven Row in 1777 traded at the sign of The Cat, which possibly owes its origin to the leopards' heads in the Weavers' arms. These are blazoned: 'Azure, on a chevron argent between three leopards' heads each having in the mouth a shuttle or, as many roses gules, seeded of the third, barbed vert'.

The Clothworkers' signs, similar to those of the Woolcombers, represented the tools of the trade and they appear on the arms of the Clothworkers' Company. 'Sable, a chevron ermine between two habicks in chief argent, and a teasel in base slipped or'. The teasel is the head or seed vessel of a species of thistle used at that time in cloth manufacture, and the habick is a trade instrument. The sign of the Ship, used by many drapers and mercers, was taken from the arms of the Company of Silkmen. These arms are 'Argent, a ship of three masts, in full sail on the sea in base, all proper; on a chief or, a bale of silk corded proper between two bundles of silk, pendent, of the last.' The supporters are camels loaded with bales of silk, and the crest a turbanned janissary guard.

The arms of the Company of Silk Throwers (the Weavers) have the turbanned janissary guards as supporters, a mulberry tree with silk worms as a crest, and are blazoned thus: 'Argent, three bundles or hanks of silk in fesse sable; on a chief azure a silk thrower's mill or.' It is from these janissary guards with their turbans that some drapers and mercers took their Turk's Head or Blackmoor's Head, though in the latter case the sign often depicts a curly headed negro and not a Moor.

The Framework Knitters do not appear to have made use of signs; perhaps they were not necessary, but the arms of the Company are interesting and worthy of inclusion here. They are blazoned: 'Argent, a knitting frame sable garnished or, with work pendent in base gules.' The supporters are 'The dexter, a student of the University of Oxford, vested proper; sinister, a woman proper vested azure handkerchief, apron, and cuffs to the gown argent, in her dexter hand a knitting needle, and in her sinister a piece of worstead-knit gules.'

The Dyers' signs were well chosen for they all represented the variety of colours possible in their work. The Peacock, The Rainbow and The Harlequin were the favourites and the Rainbow was often coupled with the Dove. John Edwards, Silk Dyer, of Aldersgate Street, had a sign which showed a dove with olive branch in its mouth flying under a rainbow on a landscape scene. The sign was called the Dove and Rainbow (*circa* 1700) and about that period there were some dozen similar signs in London. It is suggested that the sign may have come from the fact that the Dyers' Company usually performed the mystery play of the Deluge at Whitsuntide. The Green Man, still a popular public house sign, was used by the Dyers on their signboards, for example by John Parkin of East Smithfield (1720), Thomas Jefferys in Lothbury (1760) and A. and J. Boyer in Ivy Lane (1760), all of whom were London Dyers.

George Powell in Little Old Bailey in 1720 had for a sign the Dyers' Arms. These are blazoned: 'Sable, a chevron engrailed argent, between three bags madder of the last, corded or.' The madder was the principal source of dye and in Norwich a small open plain still bears the name of the Maddermarket. The plant, *rubia tinctorum*, has rough, hairy stems, small yellowish flowers, and the dye is obtained from the roots.

The Tailors were known by the sign of The Shears or often the Hand and Shears. John Harvie of Reading about 1666 showed the Shears on his token and Thomas Gill of Dartford in 1659 displayed the Hand and Shears. A well-known public house in Cloth Fair, Smithfield, was called the Hand and Shears from its association with the Tailors and Bartholomew Fair. The sign was sometimes used by the Woollen Drapers; perhaps some of them were Tailors as well, for we find that John Johnson in the Borough, Southwark, traded at the Hand and Shears in 1760 and described himself as a Woollen Draper.

The arms of the Worshipful Company of Merchant Taylors are blazoned: 'Argent, a tent royal between two parliament robes gules lined ermine, on a chief azure a lion of England.' There is no mention of the shears or the needles, which is surprising; in *London's Livery Companies* R. J. Blackham writes, 'One might expect to see scissors or needles depicted on the escutcheon of the tailor's craft, but no, the shield bears three tents and the lion of England.' No doubt in the early days, the most important part of the work of the tailor was the making of royal and knightly robes and tents and pavilions. The Robe Makers also took their sign from the Merchant Taylors' Arms, for their principal device was the Parliament or Judge's Robe, as well as the sign of The Bishop's Head.

Three Crowned Needles, which appear as a charge in the arms of the Needlemakers' Company, were used as a sign by some tailors and a London token of 1669 issued in Aldersgate by a tailor bears this device. A Robe Maker called Jacob Irish of Crediton, Devon, in the seventeenth century issued a token with the sign of the Hat and Feathers, and the Child's Coat was used by those specialising in juvenile clothing.

The Slop Sellers, where they had signs at all, often used such devices as The Jolly Sailor or The Golden Anchor. The word slops, still used in the Navy to describe clothing in general, is given two meanings in the *Shorter Oxford Dictionary*; the first is 'an outer garment, as a loose jacket, tunic, cassock, mantle, gown or smock-frock'. The second meaning clearly explains the sign of the Jolly Sailor for it reads 'ready-made clothing and other furnishings supplied to seamen from the ship's stores'. A London Clothier or Slop Seller had the sign of The

CLOTHING AND ASSOCIATED TRADES (ii)

1. Lamb and Star.
2. Indian Queen.
3. Crown and Wheatsheaf.
4. Seven Stars.
5. Device at Old Tailors' Hall, Edinburgh.
6. Eagle and Child.
7. Three Needles and Crowns.
8. Three Crowns.
9. Green Man.
10. The Feathers.
11. Angel and Star.

Minister's Gown; no doubt this particular trader specialised in making and selling gowns and clerical robes, the demand for which was quite considerable in the period in question.

The records of traders' signs do not help much in respect of the Bodice Makers, and there appears to be no mention of any particular device used by them. However, James Leech in Barbican in 1666 issued a token which shows the sign of The Cupid and Dart, and another Bodice Maker in London about 1730 was to be found at The Blue Bodice.

The sign of The Golden Glove is still a familiar one in many parts of the country. These huge metal gloves leave no doubt about the trade they symbolise, and in the seventeenth century they were one of the most common signs in any town. The usual variety of combinations was used, the Hand and Glove, the Star and Glove, the Ball and Glove, Buck and Glove or the Lamb and Glove being most frequently used.

John Stuckie of Sherborne (1659), Glover, had the sign of the Ram's Head, Thomas Shaw of Denbigh (1666) had the Goat and John Farne of Wimborne (1660) had the Glove, all these being taken from their tokens.

The arms of the Glovers' Company appeared on both tokens and signboards and were blazoned thus: 'Per fesse sable and argent a pale counterchanged, three rams salient of the second, two and one armed and unguled, or.' The crest is a ram and for this reason the Ram or the Goat was to be found on Glovers' signboards throughout the country.

The Mercers were one of the principal trades to issue tokens and the devices and emblems used were numerous. The arms of the Worshipful Company of Mercers was widely used and is blazoned: 'Gules, a demi-virgin couped below the shoulders, issuing from clouds all proper, vested or, crowned with an eastern crown of the last, her hair dishevelled and wreathed around the temples with roses of the second, all within an orle of clouds proper.'

The Golden Ball was the traditional sign of the Mercer, in particular of the Silk Mercer, and was found in conjunction with other devices such as the Blue Anchor or the Rose and Crown. The Rose and Crown may have been taken from the arms of the Company, and the Rose itself was used on the tokens of John Hill, Mercer, of Hereford (about 1666).

Birds were well represented on the Mercers' signs, for example the Three Doves of John Avery of Cranbrook, Kent (about 1666), the Black Swanne of Francis Ellerker of Paternoster Row (1664), the Eagle of Henry Carter of Blyth (about 1666) and the Eagle and Child of Ann Makepeace of Deddington (about 1666). The Hen and Chickens was used so often by Mercers that it must be regarded as one of their principal signs. The reason for this is not obvious; there seems to be no relationship between the wares of a Mercer and a Hen and Chickens. It is possible that its use as an inn sign may have come from the pelican and its nest, a bird much used in heraldry.

The Three Crowns, used by the Mercers, has an interesting origin. The device was taken by the early merchants from the arms of the City of Cologne. Similarly the White Bear came from the arms of Anne, Queen to King Richard III, who thus varied the Bear and Ragged Staff of her father the Earl of Warwick. The White Bear was the sign of Baptist Hicks, Silk Mercer in Sopers Lane End, Cheapside, who amassed a fortune selling to the courtiers of the Court of King James I and acquired a Peerage. There is no record of any other Mercer using the White Bear, though it was used by a Fan Maker, an Undertaker and a Stationer.

The sign of the Indian Queen was universally popular with the Mercers and was used, for example, by John Hartley of Water Lane (1775), Herne and Cox of High

Holborn (1766), Thomas Eaton and Son, Norwich (1844) and William Ryder, West Smithfield (about 1730).

The Indian Queen signs were all alike; they depicted a dusky queen in all her finery, followed by her retinue, a parasol held aloft and several small train bearers. The whole was set in a background which varied with the fancy of the artist; palm trees or pagodas, cotton plantations or cacti, all were possible. Indian Queens, Indian Kings, Blackboys, Blackamoors' Heads, all appeared on the signboards, and in 1730 on Ludgate Hill, a Mercer traded at the Black Boy and Comb.

The usual Lions, Stars, Suns and Angels were plentiful among the signs of the Mercers, as well as Wheatsheaves and Anchors, but none of these may be regarded as belonging especially to their trade. The Lamb was quite common but this was natural; it belonged to the Woollen Drapers in particular, but all the trades associated with cloth and clothing used it either as the Golden Fleece or the Lamb. George Robins of Buckingham (about 1667) had the sign of the Paschal Lamb and John Haskins, Mercer of Tavistock Street, London, traded at the Golden Fleece in 1760.

The choice of signs ranged far and wide with mercers and included the Babes in the Wood of Roger Gorsach of Liverpool (1672), the Mermaid of Stephen Bayly of Devizes (1668), the Three Greyhounds of Samuel Smith of Wem, Shropshire (1668) and the Pair of Hart's Horns of William Clayton of Whaley (1667). The unusual sign of the Coventry Cross used by Mercers in London was chosen no doubt because a large proportion of the silk ribbons sold by them were made in Coventry.

The Fleur de Lys was displayed by a few mercers in common with other trades; Thomas Cracroft of Burgh, Lincs. used it in 1666 and Smith, Lombard Street in 1629, traded at the Flower de Luce.

The Milliners' signs were extremely varied and it is as

well to remember that, while today we think of millinery as confined to ladies' hats and trimmings, the term had a far wider application. The dictionary definition 'a vendor of fancy wares and articles of apparel, especially of those originally made at Milan, i.e. Milan bonnets, ribbons, gloves and cutlery' gives us the reason for the apparently incongruous signboards.

The Feathers of Smith of Panton Street, London (1758), the Fan of John Souch of Oxford (1657), the Looking Glass of John Bishop of Oxford (1669) and the Acorn of Powell and Barrow of St James's Street (1766) are examples of the diversity of Milliners' signs. The token of Robert Liford of Abbington (about 1666) shows Spectacles, Scissors and Comb, not a sign perhaps but an indication of the wares of a Milliner in the seventeenth century.

The Hen and Chickens, Lamb, and Seven Stars, familiar signs in allied trades, were used in the millinery trade as well as the Hood and Scarf and the Plume of the Black Prince. The Marigold or Sunflower was a suitable choice (flowers were not widely used on signboards), and a Milliner called Nicholas Fitz Jeoffrey of the Strand displayed the Sunflower sign, while Bartholomew Hall of Chancery Lane (1668) had the Goat and Tree.

The Artichoke must be regarded as a milliner's sign but there can be no connection with the trade; possibly the novelty of it at that time had much to do with its use. In the Bagford Bills we read: 'Susannah Fordham, att the Hartichoake, in ye Royal Exchange, all sorts of fine poynts, laces, and linnens, and all sorts of gloves and ribbons, and all other sorts of millenary wares'. Lewis Harrindine of St Clements (about 1666) was both Milliner and Laceman and he traded at the Artichoke.

E. Herne, Milliner of London Bridge in 1772 traded at the Dolphin and Comb, Edward Wright of Nottingham in 1667 at the Fleur de Lys, Mary Varden of

Houndsditch at the Child's Coat and Rose in 1760, and John Toldervey of Oxford at the Unicorn in 1660. The sign of the Royal Widow in London, displayed by Matthias Otto, Jnr. in the Strand, referred possibly to Princess Augusta of Saxe-Gotha.

The Lacemen, that is the makers and sellers of gold lace, used many of the signs of the mercers and the drapers, but the Peacock or the Cock are generally regarded as traditional signs of their trade. Two well-known Lacemen in London in the eighteenth century were George Vaughan at The Golden Ball in the Strand and William Basnett at The Golden Goat, also in the Strand. In the seventeenth century we find Richard Peck at the Black Boy in Cloth Fair and Lewis Harrindine at the Artichoke in St Clements.

Although many of the Hosiers had such signs as the Fleece, the Lamb or the Woolpack, signs belonging to the woollen trade, their most common device was the Golden Leg or Golden Stocking. Gay in his *Trivia* mentions these familiar signs:

> 'On hosier's poles depending stockings ty'd,
> Flag with the slacken'd gale from side to side.'

In many cases actual stockings hung outside the shop but the more practical signs were the Golden Legs, made of wood or metal. Joseph Braban of King's Lynn (1666), Joseph Potter of Bishopsgate Street Within (1788) and Thomas Waller of the Strand (1768) all traded at the sign of the Golden Leg, whilst a Norwich Hosier of the eighteenth century had the Stocking and R, the capital R being added to distinguish it from a neighbouring business.

The sign of the Three Rabbits was universally used by the Furriers both in London and the provinces, a natural choice, for the rabbit supplied a good proportion of the fur used. James Clarke, Mercer and Furrier of Weobley (1659) and James Arnold of Cornhill (1754) both had the Three Rabbits for a sign, and the records do not provide any other sign peculiar to the trade of furrier.

The Worshipful Company of Skinners (Furriers), one of the twelve principal Companies, had as supporters to their arms a lizard or short-tailed wild cat of Norway and a marten. The arms were blazoned: 'Ermine, on a chief gules three princes' crowns composed of crosses pattee and fleur-de-lis or, with caps of the first, tasselled of the third'.

The Cap Makers' signs were mainly combination ones incorporating a cap such as the Cap in Hand, the Cap and Star and, in the case of T. Tronsdale of West Smithfield, the Fox and Cap, possibly a link with the Hunt. The Three Widows of a Dublin Cap Maker is a puzzling sign; even if it had some connection with the Three Nuns, its choice for a Cap Seller is inexplicable.

The Golden Hat, Hat and Feathers, the Gold Laced Hat and The Hat and Beaver are all typical of the signs of the Hatters, practically every one of which had a hat of some sort in the design. The Block was quite common for a Hatter's sign, that is to say the mould or block on which the hats were formed. The blocks were made of wood and when gilded made suitable signs. The Beaver hat was extremely popular in the eighteenth century and many signboards showed the Hat and Beaver. The poorer element had cloth or knitted caps, the Beaver being reserved for prosperous citizens, and even today a few of these old signs survive, for example in Frederick Street, Edinburgh.

The sign of the Three Hats was a popular device; Peter Cox of Wimborne, Dorset (1667) and Ann Gunnel of Chandoiss Street, London (1768) both used it, while in Norwich an eighteenth-century Hatter had a signboard showing six different felt hats all in a row. Among several delightful signs of London Hatters, the Hat, Bonnet and Stay of Mr. Noyes in Fore Street (1750), the Hat and

Plume of Feathers of James Weldy in Fleet Street (1760), and the Gold Laced Hat and Fame of T. F. Salter of Charing Cross (1794) are especially memorable.

The arms of the Worshipful Company of Feltmakers are very much concerned with hats and are blazoned: 'Argent, a dexter hand couped at the wrist gules between two hatbands nowed azure, in chief a hat sable banded of the third'. The crest is 'a naked arm embowed proper holding in the hand a hat sable banded azure'. The Hatters who were united with the Haberdashers in 1501 did not represent the whole trade and the Feltmakers were granted a charter by King James I.

The Charter made them all-powerful in respect of hats and felt, in fact they had the right of seizing and destroying all hats of foreign manufacture. In the *London Gazette* of March 16, 1673 is recorded the fact that they openly burnt large quantities of foreign hats in Woolchurch Market Place in London and the Market Place at Rye.

Extract from the *Norwich Mercury* of March 11, 1727:

> 'Leo Wiscard, near St Saviour's Church, in Norwich has lately come from London, a great Choice of superfine Beaver Hatts; fine Beaverets, fine Castor's and fine Carolina Beavers, and fine Cloath Hatts; fine Gray's Blue's, and fine Black Hatts, for Ladies and Gentlewomen; fine Leghorn and Bermuda Hatts, and very fine Straw Hatts, all of them being fresh made goods.'

This advertisement gives some idea of the variety of the Hatter's wares and explains why the Beaver Hat appeared on so many signboards.

The arms of the Company of Hatband Makers are blazoned: 'Azure, in a chevron between three hatbands or, as many merillions sable.'

The arms of the Company of Girdlers are blazoned as 'Per fesse azure and or, a pale counterchanged, three gridirons of the last, the handles in chief.' The crest is St Lawrence holding a gridiron and a book. At first sight it would appear that the Girdlers were the makers of Gridirons, but the prominence of this utensil in the arms is due entirely to its reference to the patron saint of the Guild, St Lawrence.

An example of a London Girdler's sign is the Whale and Raven of Joseph Lawrenson in Cheapside (*circa* 1700). The majority seemed to use general signs of the clothing trade, and not a device peculiar to the Girdlers, except in the case of the tokens where the arms were used.

VI

HABERDASHERY AND MISCELLANEOUS TRADES

Bird Fanciers, Button Makers, Chimney Sweeps, Coalmen, Coffin Plate Makers, Crutch and Bandage Makers, Fan Makers and Sellers, Gardeners, Grave Diggers, Haberdashers, Marine Store Dealers, Nightmen, Nurserymen, Pinmakers, Rat Killers, Rug Makers, Seedsmen, Stay Makers, Tent, Twine and Rope Makers, Thread Makers, Toymen, Trunk Makers, Truss Makers, Umbrella Makers, Undertakers, Whalebone Dealers

THE Button Makers, several of whom used the sign of the Golden Lion, do not seem to have had a particular device for their trade. Such general signs as the Dove, the Rose, the Queen's Head were used, and no additional evidence is obtainable from a study of the Traders' Tokens.

The Fan Makers or Fan Sellers displayed the Fan on their signboards as the principal charge, often accompanied by such additions as the Crown, the Sun, the Swan and the Seven Stars. A favourite sign was the Golden Fan and the arms of the Company of Fanmakers or Fan-stick Makers was used as well. These are blazoned: 'Or, a fan displayed, with a mount of various devices and colours, the sticks gules on a chief per pale gules and azure, on the dexter side a shaving iron over a bundle of sticks tied together or; on the sinister side a framed saw, in pale of the last.'

The arms are interesting in that they show the tools and materials of the trade, the sticks, saw and shaving iron. John Souch of Oxford, a seventeenth-century Milliner, showed a Fan on his token; possibly Fans represented an important part of his stock in trade. The Fan, the Crowned Fan, and the Two Fans were the ordinary signs of Milliners who sold fans.

In their issue of tokens, the Haberdashers made great use of the arms of the Worshipful Company, one of the twelve principal City Companies. The arms are blazoned thus: 'Barry nebulee of six argent and azure, on a bend gules a lion passant guardant or.' The supporters are two Indian goats and the Company was anciently called Hurrers and Milliners.

As befits such an important trade the signs were numerous and varied, the Buckler or the Sword and Buckler being the principal in early times. Stow's *Chronicle* mentions that in Elizabethan times 'every haberdasher then sold bucklers'. The token of Henry Holbey, Haberdasher of Norwich (1659) shows a hand holding a sword.

In the eighteenth century the principal signs of the Haberdashers were the Three Pigeons, the Sun, the Woolpack, the Falcon, the Unicorn and the Wheatsheaf. Combinations of all of these devices were used, as well as such interesting examples as the Three Protestant Queens of Thomas Small in Cheapside (1727), the Crane and Anchor of John Sage and John Gopp in Cheapside (1748), the Ape on Horseback of James Cutts in Henrietta Street (1712), and the Royal Point of Matthew Pearson in Tavistock Street (1774).

The Stay Makers, a small and specialised trade, used

the Boddice or the Pair of Stays as a sign, and both Richard Fowler of Farringdon, Berks (1669) and John Horsenail of Petersfield, Hants (1668) showed a pair of stays on their tokens. A London Stay Maker in 1692 with the initials H.S.H. used the device on his trade card, and William Mendham of Cheapside (1735) traded at the Wheatsheaf and Boddice. Other Stay Makers used signs belonging to or displayed by different sections of the clothing trade such as the Seven Stars, the Lamb and Star, the Indian Queen, and the Naked Boy.

The Whalebone Dealers, whose trade must have been closely associated with that of the Stay Makers, used the Whale as their sign. The Star and Whale and the Crown and Whale were typical examples, and a London Whalebone dealer by the name of Edward Tyson traded at the Blackmoor's Head and Whale.

Few signs are recorded as being used by the Tent, Twine and Rope Makers; their tokens usually showed a Coil of Rope as we find, for instance, with Thomas Nicholson of Boston in 1666. Naturally enough, the shipping trade was the best customer for ropes, and ships and anchors and similar devices were used as Ropemakers' signs. Heal records two London examples, the Peter Boat, and the Peter Boat and Doublet. The Peter Boat is given in the *Oxford Dictionary* as a dredgerman's double-ended boat or a local name on the Thames for a small fishing boat. The sign of William Good of London Bridge in 1668 shows a small fishing boat.

The Three Pigeons, a sign widely used by the Haberdashers, was also used by the Thread Makers. Possibly the two trades were closely connected, for even today the cottons and threads are to be found in the haberdashery department of the drapery store. The origin of the Three Pigeons is obscure; there may be a connection with the Three Doves of the Tallow Chandlers, but this seems unlikely.

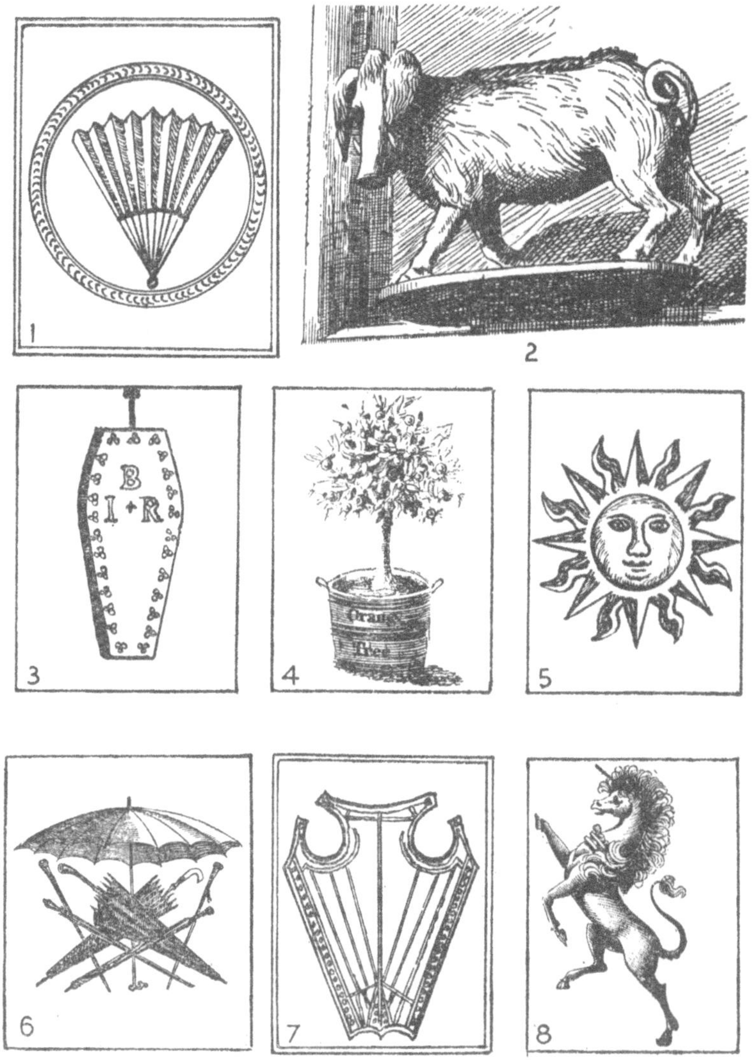

HABERDASHERY AND MISCELLANEOUS.

1. Golden Fan.
2. Golden Boar, The Mound, Edinburgh (after Fothergill). Sign of a Trunk Shop.
3. The Coffin.
4. Orange Tree—John Mason, Seedsman, 152, Fleet Street.
5. The Sun (Pinmakers).
6. Victorian Umbrella Makers' Sign.
7. The Pair of Stays.
8. The Unicorn.

The Trunk Makers, who were the makers of leather buckets as well, displayed signs directly connected with their wares. The Trunk, the Trunk and Bucket, the Two Trunks, Three Trunks, the Three Trunks and Two Buckets and many other combinations were used on their signboards.

G. A. Fothergill in 1910 records an old-established Trunk Maker in Edinburgh as trading at the Golden Boar, and a London Trunk Maker named Townsend (1760) traded at the Three Trunks and Blue Boar. William Moore of Stonegate, York (about 1666) had the sign of the Four Tobacco Pipes and possibly sold pipes as well as trunks.

The sign of the Umbrella needs no explanation and even today many of these signs exist. The umbrella came into fashion at the end of the eighteenth century, and Gay, in *Trivia*, Book I, has the phrase 'or underneath th' umbrella's oily shed' at a time when they were coming into general use.

A. N. R., writing in the *Edinburgh Evening News* of May 6, 1950, about signs, says:

> 'In Hanover Street there hangs over the heads of the pavement walkers, a parasol of gold and blue, to show all passers that here, at Gibb's, can be bought umbrellas and parasols. An umbrella hangs outside the door of Chambers, Duke Street, Leith, and a similar one in Home Street, while in Bruntsfield Place there is a gayer one.'

Hanway was the first man in London to use an umbrella and John Pugh wrote about him:

> 'When it rained a small parapluie defended his face and wig; thus he was always prepared to enter into any company without impropriety or the appearance of negligence. And he was the first man who ventured to walk the streets of London with an umbrella over his head; after carrying one near thirty years he saw them come into general use.'

There appears to be no particular sign associated with the trade of Rug Maker, and the only signs used were those associated with the woollen trade. An example of this is the token of Will Hartley of Oxford (1670), which bears the device of the Woolpack, a sign which is still common amongst the inns and taverns.

The Chimney Sweeps and Nightmen, for the two occupations were frequently combined in the old days, used the sign of the Golden Pole. Where the trade was that of a chimney sweep alone, the sign of the Sweep's Brush was used, a short sturdy turk's-head brush or the flat circular type. In the *Edinburgh Evening Dispatch* of June 6, 1941, J. W. mentions the sign of a chimney sweep who used to live in Roxburgh Place, Edinburgh, and the following lines were exhibited:

'Who lives here? Who do you think?
Joseph Rae, he loves to drink,
And if your chimney should chance to fire,
He'll put it out as you desire,
The people think it very funny
He always sweeps for ready money!'

An interesting sign in London was shown by Jeane Tempell of Nutners Street, Holborn (1740), who carried on her business at The Woman Chimbley Sweper. In 1740, women chimney sweeps cannot have been common and the title of her sign suggests that she was the only one, at least in that neighbourhood.

The Coalmen's sign was usually the Collier and Cart, sometimes the sign of the Collier alone. John Burgesse of Milford Lane, London (1666) had the sign of the Collier and Robert Farman of the same street (1668) used the Horseshoe. Thomas Williams of Strand Bridge (about 1666) displayed the Goat, Philip Fruchard of All Hallows Lane (1740) the Golden Heart and Henry Williams of Ditch Side Fleet Bridge (1760) the Three Compasses, and all of these traded as coalmen. All these Coalmen had their premises at the riverside, a reminder that all the coal of the period was waterborne. As early as 1239 Henry III gave a charter to Newcastle for liberty to dig coals, but it was not used as a fuel to any extent for many centuries. In 1577 it was written 'trade in coals beginneth to growe from the forge to the kitchen and halle in cities and towns that lie near the coast where they have little other fuel except turf and hassocke.'

The Bird Fanciers, according to their many advertisements, appear to have conducted much of their business from well-known inns. In all probability they engaged rooms for the sale of their birds as and when the imports came to hand and thus advertised at the sign of the particular inn. Larwood and Hotten mention a Bird Fancier at the sign of The Harp in the Strand, but this is the sole reference. The following advertisement of a Bird Fancier, taken from the *Norwich Mercury* of October 25, 1729 mentions the sign of The Bear, which was an inn.

> 'Just brought over from High Germany, to the Bear in the Market Place in Norwich, a fine Parcel of Canary Birds, of Various Colours: to be sold Good Pennyworths.'

The Nurserymen, Seedsmen and Gardeners naturally chose flowers, fruit and vegetables for their signs, the favourites being the Artichoke, the Pineapple and the Orange Tree. Flowers appeared on their signboards as well as the Thistle and the Acorn. John Tabor, Gardener of Norwich, in 1663 had a Spade on his token, taken perhaps from the arms of the Gardeners' Company. These are blazoned: 'The field a landscape, the base variegated with flowers, a man proper vested round the loins with linen argent digging with a spade all of the first.'

The crest is a basket of fruit and the supporters are

two emblematical female figures with a cornucopia. Two London examples are the Hand and Flower of Thomas Bailey of Covent Garden (1810) and the Thistle and Crown of James Gordon of Fenchurch Street (1768). The Orange Tree was the sign of both the Seedsmen and the Italian Merchants and the earliest record of that fruit in England occurs in the *Book of Days* in A.D. 1290.

The Rag and Marine Store Dealers had two principal signs, The Fishbone and the Black Doll. The Marine Store Dealers used to buy up old clothes, ropes and so forth from ships, surplus clothing from ships' stores, curiosities from all over the world which included carved and grotesque bones from whales and other creatures. These bones were often hung outside as a novelty to attract attention and became in time the sign of the trade, such as the Whalebone, a device which has remained as an inn sign.

The Black Doll has an interesting origin; a black doll and a pair of diamond earrings were found in a bundle of old clothes left with a dealer in Norton Folgate. The dealer waited for the diamonds to be claimed, and as no one came after some weeks, he put the black doll outside his shop to attract the attention of his customer who never came. The doll at the door rotted and was replaced by a new one, and the sign of The Black Doll came into general use.

The Naked Boy and Truss was the sign of Cornelius Glover of Three Nuns Alley, London (about 1668), and this appears to be the traditional sign of the Truss Maker. The Golden Key was another sign used by them, but as the Key belonged to the locksmiths and ironmongers it cannot be regarded as their particular sign.

The Pinmakers, whose traditional sign was the Sun, often took the arms of the Pinmakers' Company for this purpose. The arms are blazoned: 'Vert, a demi-virgin couped at the waist proper, mantled gules turned down ermine, her hair dishevelled, on her head an Eastern crown or'. The Pinmakers used some of the signs of haberdashers, which we find for example in the sign of Rowland Richardson of York (1668) who traded at the Hen and Chickens.

There are no records of signs among the Rat Killers, who had no need for them, but it is worthy of note that George Godfrey of Salisbury, Rat Killer (about 1666) issued a token which bore the figure of a rat.

The sign of the Parrot or the Green Parrot was the principal sign of the Toymen, and the Seven Stars was also widely used. The Blue Coat Boy and the Patten were both used by Toyshops and Heal records London toymen at the Three Rabbits, the Three Herrings, the Star, and the Golden Door. An interesting sign in Cheapside about 1745 was used by James Lewer who traded at the Elephant and Rising Sun.

The Coffin of the Undertaker was an unmistakable sign, for it left no doubt as to the trade of its owner. The usual variety of combinations was used, the Star and Coffin, Coffin and Crown, the Two Coffins, Three Coffins, the Four Coffins, and one of the most popular, the Naked Boy and Coffin. The trade of the Coffin Plate Chasers or Makers adopted the Angel as their sign, but one of them had the Spotted Dog on Snow Hill, London, in 1760. The Spotted Dog or Talbot Dog is the badge of the Earls of Shrewsbury, but the connection with the Coffin Plate Makers is not apparent.

The Matrons was the sign of John Bannister, Crutch and Bandage Maker of Newgate Street (about 1668), and the origin of this is not clear. It may have some affinity with the Three Nuns, but there is no evidence of this. The usual sign of the Crutch Maker was a Crutch, a simple specimen from stock, which when put above the doorway made an excellent sign of the trade.

VII

LEATHER AND FOOTWEAR

Boot and Shoe Makers, Bit and Stirrup Makers, Breeches Makers, Clogg Makers, Curriers, Harness Makers, Leather Sellers, Lorimers, Patten Makers, Saddlers, Spatterdash Makers, Spur Makers

THE sign of the Patten or the Crown and Patten indicated the Patten Maker, a trade long since vanished. The Patten was a wooden sole, used as an over-shoe to raise the shoe out of the wet mud. Gay in his *Trivia*, Book I, writes:

> 'Or underneath the umbrella's oily shed,
> Safe thro' the wet on clinking pattens tread',

and about the origin of the name he writes:

> 'The patten now supports each frugal dame,
> Which from the blue eyed Patty takes the name'.

The arms of the Patten Makers' Company are blazoned thus: 'Gules, on a chevron argent between three pattens or, tied of the second, the ties lined azure, two cutting knives conjoined sable'. The crest was also a patten.

In *The Cricket on the Hearth* we find that Mrs. Perrybingle clicked 'over the wet stones in a pair of pattens that worked innumerable impressions of the first proposition in Euclid all over the yard', while Dickens describes one of his characters in *Bleak House* 'pattening and counter-pattening in the backyard doing her household work'.

Richard Houlder of Shoreditch who was a Patten Maker in 1669, issued a token upon which he used the sign of the Press and he appears to be one of the few who did not use the Patten.

The makers of Spatterdashes, which were long gaiters of cloth or leather to protect the trousers or stockings, used them on their signs. The usual sign showed Three Spatterdashes, and such a sign in London was used by John Drakeford of the Strand in 1740.

The Bit and Stirrup Makers or Lorimers (Loriners) used the sign of the Bit or Bit and Crown, which was also a charge in the arms of the Loriners' Company. The arms are 'Azure, on a chevron argent between three manage bits or, as many bosses sable'. Similarly the Spur Makers displayed the Spur as a sign, or more often the Hand and Spur or Crown and Spur, and apart from riding spurs, silver spurs for cock fighting were made.

Both the Curriers and Leather Sellers used the Buck or the Roebuck as a sign, taken in both cases from the arms of their respective Companies. The arms of the Curriers' Company are blazoned: 'Argent, a cross engrailed or, between four pairs of curriers' shaves in saltire argent, handled of the second'. The supporters are 'The dexter, a buck proper attired and hoofed or; the sinister a goat argent armed and hoofed or'. The arms of the Leather Sellers' Company are blazoned: 'Argent, three bucks trippant reguardant gules, attired and unguled sable'. The supporters are 'The dexter a buck or, attired sable; sinister a ram argent, attired or'.

William Osborne, Leather Seller upon London Bridge traded at the Roebuck (1714), Edward Foster, Leather Seller of Panyer Alley at the Nag's Head and Gridiron (1666) and John Neatby, Currier, of Southwark, had the sign of the Roebuck in 1745.

The Breeches Makers, closely associated with the Curriers and Leather Sellers, used the sign of the Breeches and in most cases added the Buck or the Roebuck to it. The Buck and Breeches, the Glove and Breeches and the Boot and Breeches were the most common signs, and it is possible that many of the Breeches Makers made gloves and boots as well, which would account for the combination of signs.

The Saddlers' principal sign was the White Horse and the Saddle and the Stirrup were used as well. The arms of the Saddlers' Company appeared on tokens and they are blazoned thus: 'Azure, a chevron between three manage saddles complete, or'. The crest is a horse as well as the supporters and many Saddlers had a miniature White Horse hanging from a bracket above the shop. Many of these White Horses still remain; there is a fine one in Glasgow, and Claytons of Huntingdon still have a Saddle hanging outside their shop. Many of these Harness Makers had a life-size horse in the window, which served the same purpose as a tailor's dummy. They were very common in Victorian times, but today are somewhat of a rarity.

Examples in London are the Saddle Royal of Edward Ashworth in Fleet Street (1760), the Golden Stirrup of Robert Vaux in New Bond Street (1732), and the Golden Horse of Mr Ward in Westminster (1780). The following lines are the opening words of a song written for the Leather Sellers in 1822:

> 'Fourteen hundred and fourty-four Harry the Sixth
> Found the Traders in Leather most terribly mixt
> So he chose from among them the worthiest fellows
> Whom he chartered and titled the Prime Leathersellers.'

The Cordwainers, whose name later became synonymous with Shoemakers, took their name as dealers in Cordovan leather from the Spanish city of Cordova. In

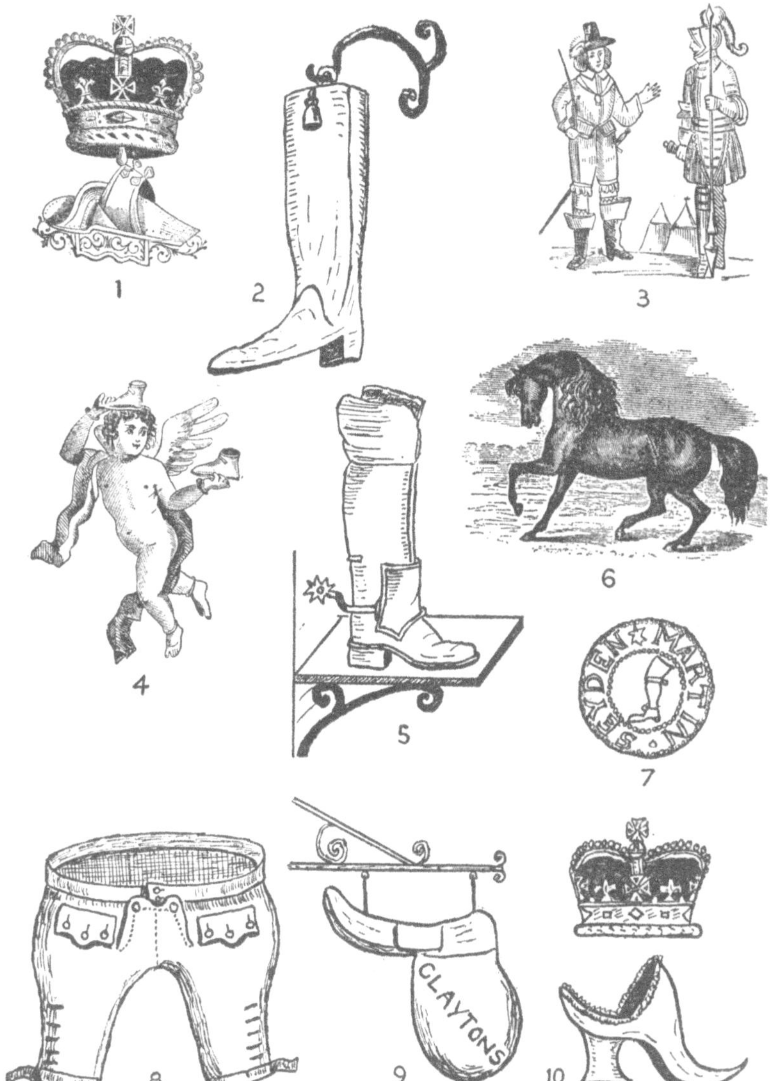

LEATHER AND FOOTWEAR.

1. Crown and Patten.
2. Golden Boot.
3. Crispin and Crispian.
4. Roman Shoemaker's Sign.
5. The Boot.
6. Black Horse.
7. Token of Martin Seyden, Bootmaker, Bury St Edmunds, 1666.
8. Breeches Maker's Sign.
9. Saddler's Sign at Huntingdon.
10. Crown and Slipper.

1409 an ordinance was passed to settle differences between 'cobblers' or workers in old leather and 'cordwainers' or workers in new leather. The arms of the Cordwainers' Company are blazoned thus: 'Azure, a chevron or between three goats' heads erased argent attired of the second.'

Their patron saint was St Crispin and he figured on many of the signboards of the Boot and Shoe Makers, in various forms such as Old Crispin, Jolly Crispin and even King Crispin. The patronal day was October 25, and in 1415 the battle of Agincourt was fought on this day, as we know well from Shakespeare's play.

Crispin and Crispian were two Roman brothers who settled in Soissons, France, and preached Christianity. They supported themselves by making shoes and sandals and about the year 287 suffered martyrdom by being thrown into a cauldron of molten lead. The sign of St Crispin was used by the Shoe Makers throughout Europe as well as in Britain.

St Hugh or St Hugh's Bones was used as a sign by the Shoe Makers, and a quotation from the *History of the Gentle Craft* (1725) mentions this and lists the tools of the period:

'My friends, I pray, you listen to me,
And mark what Saint Hugh's Bones shall be:
First a Drawer and a Dresser,
Two Wedges, a more and a lesser.
A pretty Block, Three Inches high,
In fashion squared like a die;
Which shall be called by proper name
A Heelblock, ah! the very same;
A Hand-leather and a thumb-leather likewise,
To put on Shooe-thread we must devise;
The Needle and the Thimble shall not be left alone,
The Pinchers, the Pricking Awl, and Rubbing Stone;
The Awl, Steel, and Jacks, the Sowing Hairs beside,

The Stirrop holding fast, while we sow the Cow hide;
The Whetstone, the Stopping Stick, and the Paring Knife,
All this does belong to a Journeyman's Life:
Our Apron is the shrine to wrap these Bones in,
Thus shroud we S. Hugh's Bones in a gentle lamb's skin.'

St Hugh was a prince's son, unlucky in love, who after travelling far and wide, was shipwrecked and lost his wealth. He chose the trade of shoe maker, and after his martyrdom in the reign of Diocletian his body was bequeathed to the shoe makers. They took it down from the gallows and used the bones to make tools with, hence the sign of St Hugh's Bones.

In the eighteenth century the Last, the Slipper and the Boot became the accepted signs of the trade and were used in such combinations as the Hand and Slipper, the Crown and Slipper, the Crown and Last, the Blue Last, the Boot and Crown and the Golden Boot.

On the tokens the shoe makers kept to tradition. William Greene of Nottingham had the sign of the Shoe Knife (1669), Jonathan Johnson of Ware had the Cordwainers' Arms (1666) and H. E. H. of Stanhope Street used the St Hugh's Bones (1657).

The sign of the Golden Boot was popular until the end of the nineteenth century, and indeed many remain today. There are good examples at Launceston, Edinburgh and Maidstone.

The following lines from the *Evening Dispatch* of Edinburgh dated June 6, 1941 refer to a cobbler of Inverness:

'Boots and Shoes, though nearly ended,
May be here most neatly mended;
I can make and I can mend,
I can furnish you good bend;
But Gentlemen, what do you think?
I must have the ready clink.'

These words appeared on the Cobbler's sign, in contrast to the more familiar Last.

VIII

METAL, GLASS AND OIL TRADES

Anvil Makers, Armourers and Braziers, Bell Founders, Bell Hangers, Bellows Makers, Blacksmiths, Brush Makers, Chain Makers, China Men and China Sellers, Cork Cutters, Cutlers, Glass Makers and Sellers, Ironfounders, Ironmongers, Italian Merchants, Lime Burners, Mangle Makers, Millwrights, Oil and Colourmen, Pewterers, Plumbers, Razor Makers, Smiths, Soap Makers, Sword Cutlers, Tinplate Workers, Tallow Chandlers, Tool Makers and Dealers, Wireworkers

THE trade of the Ironmonger lent itself to the provision of varied and interesting signs. Many of the signs were examples of their wares, frequently produced in their own workshops, for Ironmongery has ever been a practical craft.

On the seventeenth-century tokens, the arms of the Worshipful Company of Ironmongers were used as well as a host of assorted symbols. The arms are blazoned: 'Argent, on a chevron gules three swivels or (the middle one paleways, the other two with the line of the chevron) between three steel gads azure.'

The tokens of Daniel Bagshaw of Brassington (1663) and Robert Clayton of Norwich (1663) both show these arms, while that of James Hutchinson of Chester (1669) has the Three Doves, taken from the Tallowchandlers' Arms.

H. Muntt of Clare Street, London (1666) has the Three Candlesticks, Joseph Sylvester of Ludgate Street (1670) has a Frying Pan, Francis Bunden of Newgate Within (1666) uses the Two Crossed Keys, William Walker of Newgate Without (1666) has the Chafing Dish; S. Harrise of the Strand (about 1666) has the Lobster, and Edward Lewis of White Cross Street (about 1666) displays the Flesh Pot, and all these are taken from their tokens.

The Padlock or Golden Padlock must rank as one of the most popular of the Ironmongers' signs and it is surprising to note how many of these huge padlocks are still doing duty above their owners' shops. Messrs. C. F. Hargreaves of 4, St James' Street, Burnley, still trade at the sign of the Golden Padlock, which is a slender specimen with a very thin shackle.

Messrs. G. W. Henshall of Bury St Edmunds use this sign, which appears as well on the face of their envelopes, and which bears the words 'Ironmongery Warehouse' on the escutcheon and 'Trade Mark' on the shackle. Other Padlocks of interest belong to W. O. Waine of Nailsworth, Stroud, P. G. Fountain of Pottergate, Norwich, and Webbs of Sittingbourne, while other fine specimens may be found in Edinburgh, Daventry, Ellesmere and many towns too numerous to mention. Heal records the Padlock of Leete and Warburton of Tottenham Court Road (1838), and it would appear that these locks came into general use as signs from about the early part of the nineteenth century.

Allied to the Padlock sign is the Key or Golden Key, and many of these fine signs still remain. It was the natural choice for an Ironmonger, who was usually a Locksmith as well; and where the trader was a Locksmith only the Key was the normal sign. These huge keys were generally made of wood, with ornate bows,

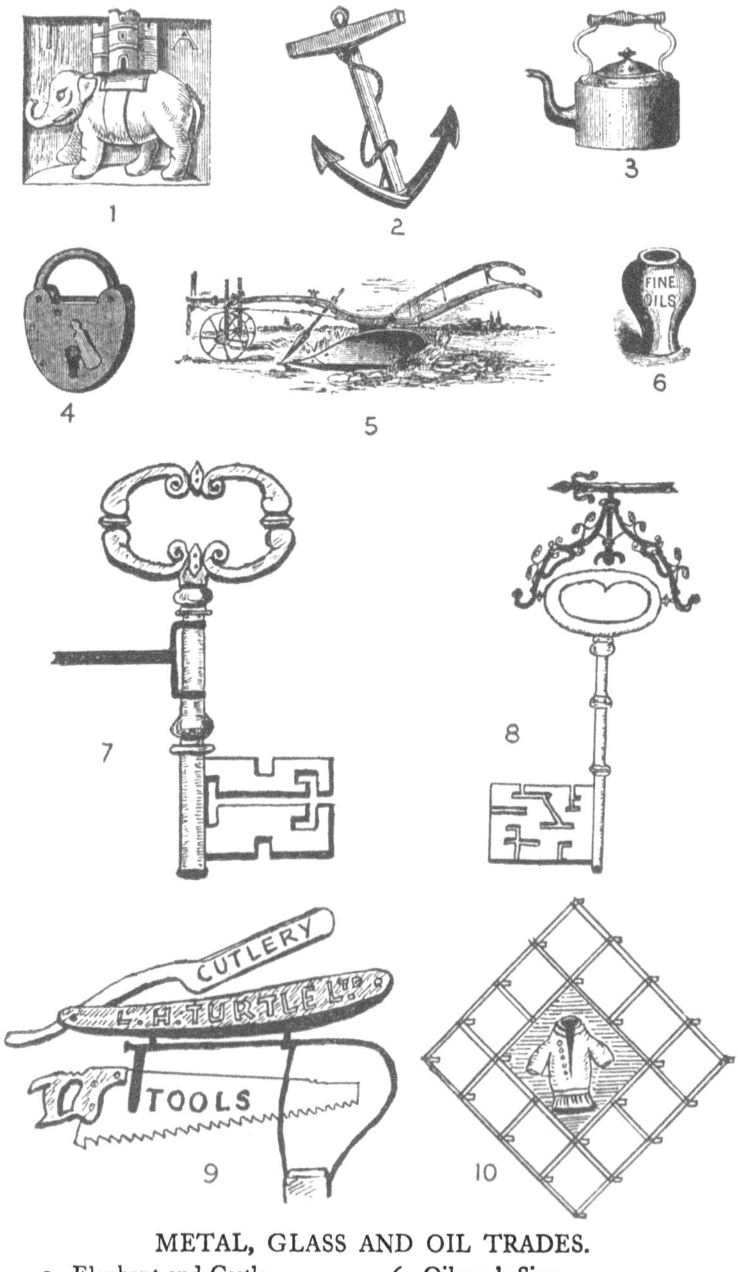

METAL, GLASS AND OIL TRADES.

1. Elephant and Castle.
2. Golden Anchor.
3. The Copper Kettle.
4. Golden Padlock.
5. The Plough.
6. Oilmen's Sign.
7. Key at Norwich.
8. Key at Chester.
9. Cutler's Sign at Croydon.
10. Harrow and Doublet.

much of the decoration being of plaster. The whole was gilded and when hung aloft looked much more solid and heavy than was actually the case.

Townsend and Crosley, Ironmongers of Gracechurch Street, London (1777) had the sign of the Three Keys, Wood and La Roche of Cheapside (1747), who were Locksmiths, had the Golden Key, and Barnard and Joy, later Barnard, Bishop and Barnard of The Walk, Norwich (founded about 1800), also had a Golden Key. This latter Key is still in existence, purchased by a neighbouring firm of Ironmongers when Barnards gave up their retail shop in about 1890.

A fine Key exists at a Whitesmith's in Watergate Street, Chester, another may be found at 40, Charlotte Street, Edinburgh, while a Tool Shop has the Crossed Keys in High Street, Edinburgh. The Crossed Keys are a common sign for Inns, taken no doubt from the arms of the Papal See. Archibald, the Ironmonger of Comiston Road, Edinburgh, is in possession of two signs for he displays not only a Golden Padlock, but a Golden Key as well, above it.

The Gridiron was another popular sign amongst Ironmongers especially in the eighteenth century, but it is not a bold sign and can be difficult to see. Heal records Thomas Buttall of the Strand (1762) at the sign of the Gridiron; while G. Jones and Sons, Ironmongers of Godalming, still display a Gridiron sign of considerable age, the premises and the business being very old indeed. A well-known business in eighteenth-century London, Thomas Hattam of the Barbican, traded at the Crossed Saws and Gridiron, and Joseph Clarke of Piccadilly (1740) used the Gridiron and Trowel.

The Copper Kettle, a sign today associated with Teashops and Cafés, was used by the Ironmongers, and these were actual kettles, made of copper, though in a size too large for domestic purposes. Evans of Colchester and

H. W. Wildman of Ledbury show kettles of this kind, and many more may be found throughout the country.

Domestic utensils were often used by the Ironmongers and Hardwaremen as signs, and the Dustpan and the Frying Pan were two of the more popular. Gabriel Nicholls of St Mary Hill, Billingsgate (1768) traded at the Frying Pan and in Islington there used to be a shop with the sign of the Illuminated Dustpan. The Family Frying Pan was an Ironmonger's sign in Highcross Street, Leicester in 1866, and in the latter part of the nineteenth century in Norwich a Hardware shop bore the name of the Little Dustpan.

In the provinces among the agricultural communities it was natural that the signs should reflect their activities, and the Golden Plough and the Golden Ploughshare were in common use by the Ironmongers. Messrs. Clay and Sons of Ellesmere, Shropshire still have a fine Plough above the doorway, and a Victorian Ironmonger's in Norwich named Stevens and Clarke had the Golden Plough in Orford Street and the Golden Ploughshare on Orford Hill. The Golden Fork, the Golden Spade, the Golden Shovel, all were used as signs; for example in 1850, William Warner traded at the Golden Shovel, 17, Tombland, Norwich.

Many other signs were used by the Ironmongers, among them the Lock and Hinge, the Anchor, and the Stove Grate; the latter sign generally took the form of a painted signboard showing the latest in grates. William Wood of Aldersgate Street (1759) traded at the Saw and Bag of Nails and surely what must be the most interesting of the lot, A. Walker of 25, Great Surrey Street, Blackfriars Road, had the sign of the Dog's Head in the Pot (1790), known locally as the Dog and Crock, the crock being another name for a cooking pot.

In the Banks collection of Bills may be found the sign of the Harrow and Doublet (dating from 1720), which hung outside an iron warehouse in Upper Thames Street, London, which in Larwood and Hotten's time was the Doublet. The sign was made of cast iron.

A firm of Ironmongers in Norwich, Palmer and Sons, traded at the Golden Pipe because in the early days they sold tobacco as well (see under the Tobacconists, page 38), while another bygone trader, J. Bertram of the Grassmarket, Edinburgh, sold ranges and grates at the Golden Ball. In Carlisle, a business which has recently closed, J. Blain in Blackfriars Street, had for a sign a giant Bass Broom which hung above the shop window.

The Tool Makers and Tool Dealers whose trade was closely connected with the Ironmongers, used everyday tools such as Saws and Planes for their signs. The Saw was the favourite and many Tool Merchants today can boast one of these signs. There is a large Handsaw at Evans and Company in the Edgware Road, London, and another may be found at L. H. Turtle of Crown Hill, Croydon. The Circular Saw is used by Frost and Barrett of St John Street, Norwich, and also at Tolbooth Wynd, Leith.

The Three Planes was the sign of John Jennison of Queen Street, London (1730), and H. Griffith of Goat Lane, Norwich had the Golden Plane (about 1820–1934), which is in the Strangers' Hall Museum in Norwich. Naturally enough the Plane Makers made their own signs for they were the stock patterns of wooden jack planes, suitably gilded.

A modern firm of Tool Merchants, W. Pond of Steelhouse Lane, Birmingham, display a variety of signs which include a Hand Saw, a Ring Spanner, an open-ended Spanner, a Key and a Hammer, all of outsize dimensions.

Many of the Tool Merchants and Ironmongers were also Cutlers, grinding and sharpening tools and cutlery as well as selling them. Huge Golden Scissors or Shears and Golden Razors were common signs, especially in

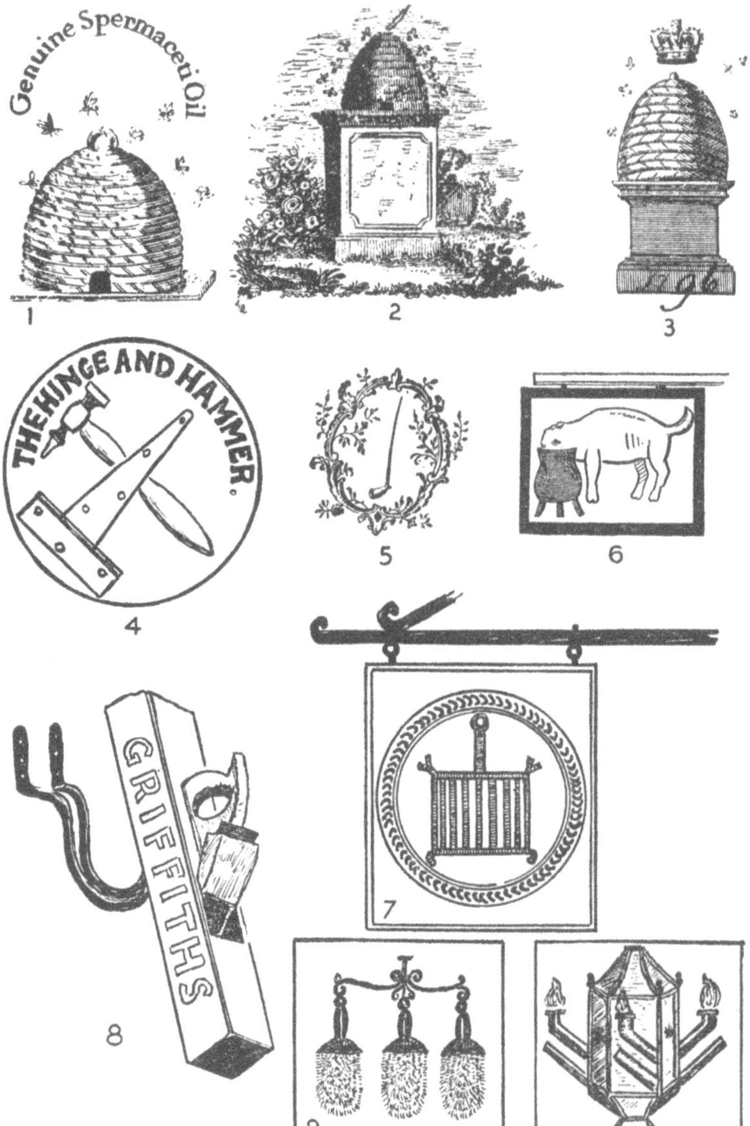

METAL, GLASS AND OIL TRADES.

1. The Beehive (1791).
2. The Beehive (1805).
3. Beehive and Crown (1796).
   (London Wax Chandlers' signs).
4. Modern Sign, London, S.E.22.
5. Golden Pipe (1601), Norwich.
6. Dog's Head in Pot
   (after Larwood and Hotten).
7. The Gridiron.
8. Golden Plane, Norwich.
9. The Three Brushes.
10. The Lamp.

Victorian times, and quite a few of these are still in evidence. An example of this is the Scissors of C. W. Brown of Church Street, Croydon and the Razor of L. H. Turtle of Crown Hill, Croydon. A Cutler in Perth has a large open Razor, another Cutler in Tiverton has what must be the largest Knife and Fork on record. These latter signs stand one each side of an upstairs window on a corner site and are most effective.

The Cutlers, Sword Cutlers and Razor Makers of earlier days were craftsmen in the sense that they made the goods that they sold and their signs were varied and colourful. On their tokens in the seventeenth century they used the arms of the Cutlers' Company which are blazoned thus:

'Gules, three pair of swords in saltire argent, hilts and pommel or, viz. two pair in chief and one in base.' The crest is the Elephant and Castle and the supporters are elephants. The token of Robert Douglas of Norwich (1656) had the Crossed Swords, that of George Bishop of Oxford (1668) had the Crossed Swords and Elephant's Head, and Humphrey Taft of Chancery Lane (1665) used the Anchor and Sword.

The Sword Cutlers used the Crossed Daggers, the Crossed Swords, the Sword Erect, and the Flaming Sword as their particular signs, whereas the general Cutlers had the Case of Knives, usually found in combination with other devices such as the Star, the Unicorn, the Anchor and the Lion.

The Armed Elephant or the Elephant and Castle was used as a sign, taken from the crest of the Cutlers' Company, and today many inns still use this device. It is believed that the Cutlers adopted the elephant in reference to the ivory used by them for handles. P. Savigny, Cutler in St Martin's Churchyard in 1700, had the sign of the Crown and Halbert, and T. Bickerstaff in Princes Street used the Halbert, this particular device being associated with the Surgical Instrument Makers. Many of the Cutlers' signs and billheads incorporated their Cutlers' Mark or Trade Mark and the history of these Marks is bound up with that of their signs.

The arms of the Worshipful Company of Tinplate Workers and Wireworkers provided the Tinmen with their most popular signs, the Lamp, or the Lamp and Crown. These arms are blazoned thus: 'Sable, a chevron or, between three lamps (the two in chief, one light each facing each other, the lamp in base with two lights) argent garnished or, illuminated proper.' The crest is 'a globular ship lantern, or lamp, ensigned with a regal crown proper'. The supporters are 'Two working tinmen proper, vested in blue coats with red cuffs, lined with fur, blue breeches, red waistcoat, white stockings, black shoes, and silver buckles, and on the head a fur cap'.

John West of Snow Hill (1668) had the sign of the Crown, Henry Kemp of the Strand used the Lamp and Crown (1760) and Jonathan Tudway of Charing Cross had the Three Lamps (1756), all of which were taken from the Company arms.

An interesting sign of a London Tinman named Bevington of Lombard Street (1760) was the Golden Teakettle and Speaking Trumpet. Tinmen also used the sign of the Teapot itself in a similar manner to the Ironmongers with the Kettle. Any Victorian catalogue of the trade will show quite a large variety of Tinplate Teapots, and the China Men or Earthenware Dealers used this sign as well. In Norwich today a China Dealer named Nickalls has a large silhouette Teapot hanging outside his shop in the Market Place.

The other signs of the China Men were the China Jar (generally of oriental design), the Canister, and the Flower Vase or Flower Pot. The China Jar sometimes appeared as the Golden Jar, in distinction to the Jars of the Oilmen which were painted red or green.

The sign of the Wireworker was generally the Bird Cage, a far more elaborate affair than is common today, and to distinguish it from the signs of competitors other devices were added. One Wire Drawer named John Ruduck issued a token bearing the device of a Catherine Wheel, which is a charge in the arms of the Turners' Company.

The Pewterers' signs were few, mainly the Pewter Dish, the Golden Dish and the Black Boy and Worm. The Worm was a long winding pewter pipe used in distilling and was taken from the arms of the Pewterers' Company. These are blazoned as 'Azure, on a chevron or, three antique limbecks argent, as many roses gules seeded of the second, barbed vert.' The crest is two arms holding a dish and the supporters are seahorses. The limbecks were antique stills and must have played an important part in the trade of the Pewterer to have appeared as a charge in the arms.

The Glass Makers used the sign of the Golden Bottle, the Bottle appearing as a charge on the arms of the Glass Sellers' Company and the Company of Bottle-Makers and Horners. The arms of the latter Company are blazoned: 'Argent, on a chevron between three leather bottles sable, as many buglehorns stringed of the first'.

Naturally the Glass Sellers used a representation of a Glass Bottle on their signboards, whereas the bottle of the Bottle-Makers' Company was made of leather, and in England leather black jacks remained in use long after glass vessels had become common on the Continent.

The Anvil Makers, using the sign of the Anvil and Crossed Hammers, had it in common with the Blacksmiths. The latter naturally used the tools of their trade and the anvil and hammers were the most important part. The arms of the Blacksmiths' Company were frequently used as signs and the blazon runs: 'Sable, a chevron or, between three hammers argent, handled of the second, ducally crowned of the last'.

1

2

3

4

5

6

7

METAL, GLASS AND OIL TRADES.

1. Ironmonger's Trade Card (1780).
2. Norwich (1880).
3. National Institute of Hardware.
4. Anvil Maker.
5. Colophon of the Ironmonger (Trade Journal).
6. Coppersmith's Trade Card (1852).
7. Golden Pipe (1880).

A token issued by Nicholas, smith of Chappell Frith in 1671 shows an Anvil, but 'Robert Unwen in Dore in Darbysheir' displayed a Hammer and Tongs. The Blacksmiths, who were generally Farriers as well, sometimes used a Horse's Head as a sign, and Fothergill records a fine Gilded Head made of iron at Leith Walk, Edinburgh, though in this case it indicated a Saddler.

Horse Shoe signs were to be found in plenty, usually in the form of the Three Horseshoes, taken no doubt from the Farriers' Arms, blazoned thus: 'Argent, three horseshoes sable, pierced of the field'. This sign has persisted as an Inn Sign and in practically every rural district today one inn at least is known as the Three Horseshoes.

The Smiths with an agricultural connection often displayed a Plough or a Harrow as a sign, though with their type of craft no sign was really necessary. The general Smiths in the town often displayed a Lock and Hinge or a Smoke Jack. These revolving mechanical jacks were fine examples of the smith's art. Many examples exist in our folk museums and a representation of one of these as a trade sign was most appropriate.

The Millwrights were another body of craftsmen who displayed little or nothing in the way of signs, but here and there a picture of a Mill was used or else the tools of their trade, or parts of the mill machinery. The Mill was often shown as a Windmill or else as a Hand Mill, and in the latter case a man is generally shown turning it.

For the Mangle Makers there was only one possible sign and practically all of them traded at the sign of the Mangle. These were naturally very different from the compact and efficient machines of today for they were both bulky and heavy to work. In the closing chapters of *Nicholas Nickleby* the once dashing Mr Mantalini is found to be employed in a cellar, turning the handle of one of these monsters, known as box mangles and filled with stones. One of these machines in a museum has the following lines above it:

'Turn away at the Mangle, Joe,
And you shall have a kiss,
Do turn away at the Mangle, Joe,
Six dozen after this,
Turn away at the Mangle, dear,
You are my heart's delight,
And I will see what father says,
When he comes home tonight.'

The Bell Founders, always a small and select craft, had little need for signs, but a well-known example is the Three Bells of the famous Whitechapel foundry which was founded in 1700 and is still in existence.

Very little can be found about the Bellows Makers but it is known that some of them had a pair of Bellows above the door, while the Chain Makers do not seem to have bothered about signs at all. The only example that appears to be recorded is given by Heal in his *Signboards of Old London Shops*. This is of Henry Price at the Two Chains and Buckle in King's Gate Street in 1770.

The Armourers and Braziers either used the tools of their trade or devices closely associated with it for their signs. For example, Peter Deale, Armourer, of Norwich (1664) had the sign of the Helmet, and Richard White, Brazier, of Cliff, Sussex (1668) had the Hammer. The arms of the Worshipful Company of Armourers are blazoned: 'Argent, on a chevron sable a gauntlet of the first between two pairs of swords in saltire of the last, hilts and pommels or, on a chief of the second an oval shield of the field, charged with a cross gules encircled with a carved shield of the third between two peers' helmets proper garnished or.'

The arms of the Worshipful Company of Braziers is blazoned: 'Azure, on a chevron or, between two ewers in chief, and a three-legged pot with two handles in base of the second, three roses gules seeded or, barbed vert'. The Braziers were incorporated with the Armourers by Queen Anne and the arms were joined; the Armourers are borne on the dexter side of the escutcheon, impaling on the sinister the ensigns of the Braziers.

The Braziers had a variety of signs, one of which, the Ewer or Golden Ewer, was taken from their arms. The Frying Pan, the Cross Keys, the Tea Kettle, and the Golden Bell were all typical signs, as well as the Chamber Grate and Gridiron of Thomas Stevenson of Houndsditch (1745) and the Two Candlesticks and Key of Thomas Doxey, Without Bishopsgate (1771).

Though it is quite possible that the Plumbers found the need for signboards in common with other tradesmen, there is very little information concerning them. The arms of the Company of Plumbers (incorporated in 1612) are most interesting, the tools of their trade appearing as charges. The arms are blazoned: 'Or, on a chevron sable between a cross staff fesseways of the last, enclosed by two plummets (plumb lines) azure, all in chief, and a level reversed in base of the second, two soldering irons in saltire, between a cutting knife on the dexter, and a shave hook on the sinister, argent'. The crest is 'A triple fountain or, issuing water proper, on the top an angel of the last, vested argent, ducally crowned and winged of the first, holding in the dexter hand a sword, and in the sinister a pair of scales, both or'.

Similarly the Ironfounders are not credited with the use of signs, though in many cases the early Ironmongers had small foundries, particularly those who sold grates, many of whom had the Stove Grate on their signboards. The arms of the Company of Founders are blazoned: 'Azure, a laver pot between two taper candlesticks or'. The crest is unusual for it is almost a complete picture of the Ironfounder at work. 'A fiery furnace proper, two arms of the last issuing from clouds on the sinister side of the first, vested azure holding in both hands a pair of closing tongs sable taking hold of the melting pot in the furnace, proper.'

The Oilmen or the Oil and Colourmen had two principal signs, the Olive Tree and the Oil Jar. The Olive Tree, source of much of their oil, was a natural choice, and the tall earthen vessels which contained this oil made suitable signs in themselves. Many of these jars remain today outside oil and colour shops, generally painted green, such as those above Mence Smith's shop in Folkestone or at Lord Hill's Road, London, W.2.

The Neats' Tongues, another sign belonging to the oil trade, are interesting for they symbolise neat's-foot oil, obtained from the feet of oxen. The word Neat is now rarely used of cattle, though neat's-foot oil is still used. John Baker of Fenchurch Street had the sign of the Three Tongues (about 1669), and John Lyde in the Strand conducted his oil business at the sign of the Three Neats' Tongues.

On the tokens of the Oilmen several different signs appeared such as the Dragon of Joseph Hast, Without Temple Bar (about 1666), the Three Tuns of William Parker of Mark Lane (1669), the Three Arrows of John Amyes of Leadenhall Street (about 1666), and the Sunflower and Sun of Joseph Man of The Savoy (1667).

The Good Woman, The Silent Woman and the Quiet Woman were all used by Oilmen to represent their trade and the picture showed a woman without a head. The sign has survived with the inns and taverns, but its origin is open to speculation. The most likely origin is the link with the heedless (punned to make headless) or foolish virgins of the parable who had no oil in their lamps when the bridegroom came.

The Italian Merchants or Warehousemen used the Olive Tree, the Oil Jar and the Neats' Tongues of the Oilmen. Possibly some of them were engaged in both trades, and the Olive Tree would be a suitable device to represent things Italian. Similarly they used the Orange Tree as a sign, but there is no record of this being used for an oilman, only for an Italian Merchant or a Toyman.

The Colourmen had few distinctive signs; the Harlequin, the Golden Palette and the Colour Barrel were the most usual. The Olive Tree and Colour Barrel of James Stone, Within Bishopsgate in 1760, is interesting; possibly he was both oil and colourman.

The Wax Chandlers, producers of the finest candles for religious purposes, the main ingredient of which was beeswax, naturally chose the Beehive as their particular sign. The usual varieties were to be found, such as Star and Beehive, the Crown and Beehive, the Golden Beehive, and Heal records the Beehive and Wax Chandler of Lewis Dupuis in Beake Street, London, 1771. The arms of the Wax Chandlers' Company are blazoned thus: 'Azure, on a chevron argent between three mortcours (lamps) or, as many roses gules seeded of the third, barbed vert'. These arms appeared on their tokens to some extent, but the Beehive was the more popular device.

The Tallow Chandlers, whose fraternity produced the cheaper tallow candles for domestic purposes, also used their arms on tokens and examples are numerous. The arms are blazoned: 'Per fesse azure and argent a pale counterchanged, three doves of the last, each holding in the beak an olive branch or'. The supporters are angels and the crest includes a dish upon which rests the head of St John the Baptist, their patron saint.

A large number of tokens show the manufacture of tallow candles and illustrate clearly the various moulds used. Apart from the manufacture of candles, the Tallow Chandlers sold a variety of associated wares such as soaps, oils, pots and pans and brushes, in fact many of the items that we associate today with Chandlery.

Larwood and Hotten record the sign of Castor and

Pollux for T. & J. Bolt, Tallow Chandlers of Berners Street, off Oxford Street, and the illustration shows Castor and Pollux dressed as Roman soldiers standing near a cask of tallow. Daniel Naler of Holborn (1662) had the sign of the Three Stags, James Miller of Tothill Street (about 1666) the Fleur de Lys, Samuel Elce of Barbican the Three Crowns, but none of these are particular to the Chandlers.

The Soap Makers have few signs to their credit, but the Dolphin was a traditional one taken from the arms of the Soap Makers' Company. These were blazoned: 'Azure, a dolphin naiant, between three eel-spears or'. An interesting advertisement is taken from the *Domestic Intelligencer* of January 2, 1679: 'William Deval, at the Angel and Stilliards, in St Ann's Lane, near Aldersgate, London, maketh Castle (Castille), Marble, and white Sope as good as any Marseilles Sope; Tryed and Proved and sold at very Reasonable Rates'. An unusual sign of a Soap Maker in Norwich was used by Major Long at the Hand and Golden Scummer, the scummer being the shallow ladle or sieve used to skim off the impurities from the liquid soap. The Whale and Three Harpoons was the sign of Thomas Leader of Ratcliff Highway (1667), and the Horse and Groom was displayed by James Smith of St John Street, both London Soap Makers.

The only evidence of signs used by the Lime Burners is taken from the tokens issued in the seventeenth century but this does not prove that signs hung outside their premises. On the token of Samuel Irons, Lime Burner of Purfleet in 1669, is a representation of a Lime Kiln, and that of an unknown issuer in Millbank about 1666 shows a Lime Man carrying a sack.

The Cork Trade appears to have only one sign, the Cork Tree, a rarity in itself, for few examples are known, and Heal records but one for London, that of John Purser in St Andrew's Street, Seven Dials in 1760. The same authority mentions also a Cork Jacket Maker at the sign of the Cork Jacket, and this particular sign is the only one of its kind recorded. The representation of the Cork Tree is similar to that of an oak, the Cork-Oak from which the bark is taken being the *Quercus Suber.*

The Brush Makers were in the happy position of being able to make their own signs, for many of these were extra large brushes, made on the premises. The type of brush displayed was a pattern which even today is still called a Turk's Head, and a common sign was the Three Brushes, arranged sometimes side by side, but more often in a pyramid. Both the Two Brushes and the Four Brushes were known in eighteenth-century London, and a Norwich Brush Maker named Cook used to have a single large turk's head brush above the doorway.

A bygone Brush Maker in Kendal, Westmorland, has left a fine though aged sign in the form of a Boar. The sign would properly be styled the Wild Boar, and it is from this animal that the finest bristle used in brush-making is obtained. The Kendal Boar is made of wood and his bristles are made of bass, that sturdy fibre which is used for making stiff brooms for sweeping yards and roads. The Wild Boar now stands guard over a Grocer's shop which occupies the site of the brush factory, not entirely out of place when one remembers the bacon in the window.

IX

BUILDING AND FURNITURE

Bricklayers, Cabinet Makers, Carpenters, Coachmakers, Coopers, Feathermen, Glaziers, Masons, Measure Makers, Paviors, Sculptors, Shipwrights, Turners, Upholsterers, Woodmongers

THE Carpenters, who in Roman times used the tools of their trade, the Saw, Adze and Chisel, as a sign, frequently displayed the arms of the Worshipful Company in the seventeenth and eighteenth centuries. These arms are blazoned: 'Argent, a chevron engrailed between three pairs of compasses, extended, sable.'

Amongst the present-day inn signs, the Carpenters' Arms is still quite common, and the County of Norfolk alone can provide fourteen. Many carpenters in the old days hung miniature coffins outside their workshops, for coffin-making was quite an important part of their trade and provided them with a sign which was easy to recognise.

The Woodmongers do not appear to have many signs to their credit for they are not mentioned in previous works. They did issue tokens in the seventeenth century, and from these four different signs can be recorded. Ralph Fancott of Millbank displayed Robin Hood and Little John, Peter Tull of Cousin Lane traded at the Plough, Richard Fisher of Millbank at the Crooked Billet and John Clay of Whitefriars at the Horse and Cart, all of these in the London area.

The Measure Makers, who were generally craftsmen in wood, naturally enough used a measure for a sign. The Standard Bushel was the sign, and we know that in 1790 in Eastcheap a Measure Maker traded at the Golden Standard Bushel.

The signs of the Coopers were usually home-made examples of their craft and as such unmistakable. The Cask, the Bathing Tub and the Pail were all to be found, very few if any being left today. In Norwich the last Cooper, Clarke of Ber Street, closed down in 1954 and his sign, the Cask, was removed from above the doorway. The arms of the Worshipful Company have been known to appear as a sign and these are blazoned: 'Gyronny of eight, gules and sable, on a chevron between three annulets or, a grose between two adzes azure; on a chief vert, three lilies slipped, stalked and leaved argent.' The adze was one of the principal tools, the annulets are heraldic circles signifying the hoops and the grose was a special type of nipper.

The Coach Makers or Coach Builders often used the sign of a Wheel, a simple device which was highly suitable for their trade. A Victorian Coach Builder in Norwich, Addison by name, worked at the Golden Gig Wheel, and at Good Easter an inn had the name of The Wheelers' Arms. These were blazoned: 'Gules, a chevron between three wheels or, on a chief argent, an axe lying fessways proper.' The Compasses often appeared on Coach Makers' signs and Heal quoted John Edwards of Fleet Ditch, near Holborn Bridge, in 1717 as having the sign of the Old Collier and Cart.

The arms of the Coachmakers' and Coach-Harness Makers' Company are blazoned: 'Azure, a chevron between three coaches or,' and the crest is Phoebus driving the chariot of the sun, the supporters being two horses.

The Plasterers or Plaisterers do not seem to have provided us with much in the way of signs. An example in London is Thomas Brown at the Golden Head (the same sign as Sculptors and Masons) in Ax Yard, Westminster in 1770. The Trowel and Hammer, a common inn sign, is probably taken from the arms of the Plaisterers' Company, which are blazoned thus: 'Azure, on a chevron engrailed or, between two plaisterers' hammers and a trowel, argent in chief, hammers handled of the second, and a treble flat brush in base of the third, handled of the fourth, a rose gules seeded or, barbed vert, between two fleurs-de-lis of the first.'

The arms of the Glaziers appear on some of their tokens and are blazoned: 'Two grozing irons in saltire between four closing nails; on a chief a lion passant-guardant.' The grozing iron was one of their principal tools, used as a kind of nippers. The sign of the Sash was used in London; two seventeenth-century examples are Edward Marshall in King Street, Seven Dials, and Edward Thornton in Old Bedlam, Moorfields.

Isaac Cowper of Norwich in 1666, Bricklayer, traded at the sign of the Trowel, but there seems to be little evidence of the general use of signs by this trade. The Bricklayers' Arms are blazoned: 'Azure, a chevron or, in chief a fleur-de-lis argent between two brick axes palewise of the second; in base a bundle of laths of the last.' These arms may have been used as a trade sign (they appear commonly as inn signs), but this cannot be proved from the records.

The Sculptors and Masons were often to be found at the sign of the Golden Head. The head was sometimes nameless and at other times bore the name of some classical or historical figure. This applied mainly to the Sculptors, for the Masons engaged in the building trade used the Compasses as a sign, taken no doubt from the Masons' arms which are 'Sable, on a chevron between three towers argent, a pair of compasses, open, of the first.' A firm of Sculptors in London in 1780, Vino and Peronne of High Holborn, traded at the Golden Vase, another traditional sign.

The arms of the Turners' Company are blazoned as follows: 'Azure, a catherine wheel between two columns or; in chief a regal crown proper; in base an axe argent, handled of the second, lying fesseways, the blade downwards.' The crest is St Catherine holding a catherine wheel and a sword. These arms were used as signs, for example by Robert Stent in Little Britain in the early part of the eighteenth century. St Catherine, their patron saint, was adopted as a sign as well as articles of their craft such as Coffee Mills and Rocking Horses. The sign of the Rocking Horse is interesting, probably confined to the trade or craft of Turner.

Chairs, Cabinets and Looking-Glasses all appeared on the signs of the Cabinet Makers. The Walnut Tree, one of their principal sources of raw material, was quite common on signboards, appearing alone or in combination with various articles of furniture. In Edinburgh a Cabinet Maker called Reoch traded at the Golden Chair, which was also the sign of William Kirk in the Strand in 1749. Chippendale himself used the sign of the Chair at his shop in St Martin's Lane in 1756, while John Burrough, Cabinet Maker to Charles I, worked at the Looking-Glass on Cornhill. Many Cabinet Makers displayed a White Swan and the reason for this is not obvious though it may have been connected with the use of swansdown.

The trade of Upholsterer was closely connected with that of the Cabinet Maker, and in some cases their signs were similar. The traditional sign was the Tent or Three Tents taken from the arms of the Upholders' Company. These are blazoned: 'Sable, three pavilions ermine, lined azure, garnished or; within the pavilion in base a lamb

1

2

3

4

5

6

7

8

9

BUILDING AND FURNITURE.

1. Cooper's Sign.
2. The Griffin and Chair.
3. Victorian Cooper's Billhead.
4. Victorian Furnisher's Billhead.
5. Upholsterer's Tent.
6. Masons' Tower.
7. Turners' Catherine Wheel.
8. Victorian Shipwright's Bill-head.
9. Carpenters' Arms.

couchant argent on a cushion or, tasselled of the last; over the head a cross pattee fitchee gules.'

In Edinburgh, William Murray was to be found at the Royal Tent; in London, Robert Webb at the Queen's Head and Three Tents (1716), and Cecil Pitt at the Royal Tent in Moorfields (1763). As with the Cabinet Makers, so the Upholsterers chose examples of their wares for their signboards, Cushions, Curtains and Beds were the most popular.

The Bed usually appeared as the Royal Bed, the Cushion was combined with the Crown, and the Curtains took a colour such as the Blue Curtain of Johnathan Fall of St Paul's Churchyard (1763). The Three Crickets in Crooked Lane seems an odd choice for a London Upholsterer, but when it is remembered that the Crickets were in fact small stools the device appears suitable.

The Feathermen and the Feather-Bed Men whose trade was allied to that of the Upholsterer, have few recorded signs; there was the Angel in London and provincial examples of the Swan are known.

The Paviors are one of the trades that found no use for signs at all, the very nature of their work made signboards unnecessary. The arms of the Paviors' Company are included for reference and are blazoned thus: 'Argent, a chevron between three flagstones sable.' The crest is 'An arm enbowed, vested azure, cuff argent, holding in the hand proper a pickaxe of the last.' The motto is unusual: 'God can raise to Abraham children of stones.'

The Shipwrights used few signs. Here and there such examples as the Noah's Ark or the Adze were to be found, and where a Ship appeared on a signboard it was often above a Mercer's or Draper's shop (except, of course, outside the many taverns). The Ark appears in both the crest and arms of the Company of Shipwrights, which are blazoned thus: 'Azure, on an antique hulk, the stern terminating with the head of a dragon; in the hulk the ark, with three doors in the side; from the ark, against the side, a stip-ladder all or, on a chief argent the cross of St George gules, charged on the centre with a lion passant guardant of the second.' The crest is 'An ark as in the arms or, on the ground vert; on the top of the ark a dove argent holding in the beak an olive branch vert.'

X

ARTISTS AND OPTICIANS, AND MISCELLANEOUS TRADES

Artists, Bowyers, Clock and Watch Makers, Carvers and Gilders, Engravers, Fishing Tackle Dealers, Fletchers, Gold Beaters, Gunsmiths, Instrument Makers, Marriage Mongers, Marriage Insurance Offices, Map and Chart Makers and Sellers, Musicians, Musical Instrument Makers, Music Sellers, Opticians, Painters and Paper Stainers, Playing Card Makers, Pencil Makers, Scale Makers, Scriveners and Writing Masters, Taxidermists

THE Playing-Card Makers had the perfect subject for a sign in their own productions, and though many different cards were used the favourites were Court cards, the Knave of Clubs, King of Diamonds and the Queen of Hearts especially.

A billhead is preserved in the Banks collection of Edward Hall of Piccadilly, Playing-Card Maker to Queen Anne, whose sign was the Merry Andrew. The name is said to have come from Doctor Andrew Borde, a sixteenth-century writer and physician, whose witticisms were renowned. He wrote the *Merry History of the Miller of Abingdon*, the *Merry Tales of the Wise Men of Gotham*, and his many imitators were labelled 'Merry Andrews.'

The arms of the Company of Cardmakers are blazoned: 'Gules, on a cross argent between the four ace cards proper (viz the ace of hearts and diamonds in chief, the ace of clubs and spades in base), a lion passant guardant of the first.' The crest is an arm holding the ace of hearts.

In some of the early packs of cards the King of Clubs represented the Pope; the King of Spades the King of France; of Diamonds, the King of Spain; and of Hearts, the King of England. The spades stood for the soldiers, the clubs for the husbandmen, diamonds for the artisans, and hearts for the ecclesiastics.

The Company of Painter-Stainers represented a fusion of two guilds, the Painters and the Paper Stainers. The arms of the Company are blazoned: 'Quarterly, first and fourth, azure, three escutcheons argent, two and one; second and third, azure, a chevron between three phoenix heads, erased or.' The crest is a phoenix and the supporters are two leopards.

The signs of the Paper Stainers were few; the two main devices that they employed were the Rainbow and the Phoenix. On the other hand the Painters, with whom must be included the Artists, had a wide range of subjects, naturally enough when it is remembered that they were responsible for the production of many of the signs for the tradesmen.

The principal signs of the Painters were the Golden Head, the St Luke's Head, the Golden Palette, and often the King's Arms. The Golden Head generally represented a classical hero or author, or else a well-known person of the period.

In Nichols' *Anecdotes of Hogarth* the following appears concerning the Golden Head type of sign:

'Hogarth made one essay in sculpture. He wanted a sign to distinguish his house in Leicester Fields; and thinking none more proper than the Golden Head, he, out of a mass of cork, made up several thicknesses compacted together, carved a bust of Van Dyke, which he gilt and placed over his door. It is long since decayed, and was succeeded by a head of Sir Isaac Newton.'

It was here in 1735 that Hogarth published the 'Harlot's Progress'.

Many portraits of St. Luke were used by painters on their signboards. He was the patron saint of their guild and the fraternity had existed well before 1283.

The Scriveners and Writing Masters had three signs, all closely allied, which were the Golden Pen, the Hand and Pen, and the Hand and Golden Pen. Peter Bales, the Penman of Queen Elizabeth, after winning a golden pen in a contest, set up as his sign the Hand and Golden Pen.

T. Cooke of St Paul's Churchyard (1710) traded at the Two Golden Pens, while in Petticoat Lane there existed the sign of the Five Inkhorns, but this may have belonged to a maker of inkhorns. The Hand and Pen was used as a sign by the Fleet Street Marriage Mongers.

The Marriage Insurance Offices, of which there were many in the early eighteenth century, used the sign of the Hand and Heart, and one such office in Newgate conducted its business at the Golden Candlestick.

The sign of the Hand and Pencil indicated a Pencil Maker. Two such were Elizabeth Andrews in Houndsditch in 1770 and William Baylis in Bride Lane in 1748.

Atlas, the traditional upholder of the world, was chosen by Joseph Moxon of Cornhill in the seventeenth century as his sign, and most of his brother Map and Chart Makers and Sellers used similar devices. John Thornton, the Hydrographer to the East India Company, had the sign of England, Scotland and Ireland at his premises in the Minories in 1673.

The Carvers and Gilders used similar signs, in many cases, to those of the Painters and Artists. The Golden

Head was by far the most common, possibly because it represented their craft and the type of work that they carried out. They made a large proportion of the signs, and as the majority were gilt, it stood for a major share of their trade. An interesting sign was that of Henry Jouret, in Grafton Street, Soho, who traded at the Architrave Frame (about 1760).

The Carvers came under the jurisdiction of the Joiners' Company, whose arms are blazoned as follows: 'Gules, a chevron argent between two pairs of compasses, in chief, extended at the points, and a sphere in base or, on a chief of the last a pale azure between two roses gules seeded of the third, barbed vert, on the pale an escallop shell of the second.' The crest is a demi-savage holding a spear and the supporters are two naked boys, one of whom holds a joiner's square.

The Taxidermists had little need for signs, in that their windows, full of stuffed birds, animals and fish, served the purpose. In Norwich, however, T. E. Gunn, late Sayer of St Giles' Street, traded at the Golden Butterfly until a few years ago. This Taxidermist's sign was fortunately saved and can be seen in the Strangers' Hall Museum in Norwich.

The Fishing Tackle Dealers often availed themselves of the skill of the Taxidermist to provide signs in the shape of huge stuffed fish, generally to be found hanging in the doorways. The traditional signs were the Fish and Crown, the Golden Fish, the Angler and Trout and the Compleat Angler.

The two latter signs were generally of a landscape nature showing a fisherman by a river bank, whereas the Golden Fish was usually a large model. Modern dealers in Fishing Tackle often have a large coloured Float above the shop such as the one in Regent Road, Great Yarmouth or A. C. Browne of Timberhill, Norwich, while at East Looe in Cornwall a Barrel is the sign. Mention must also

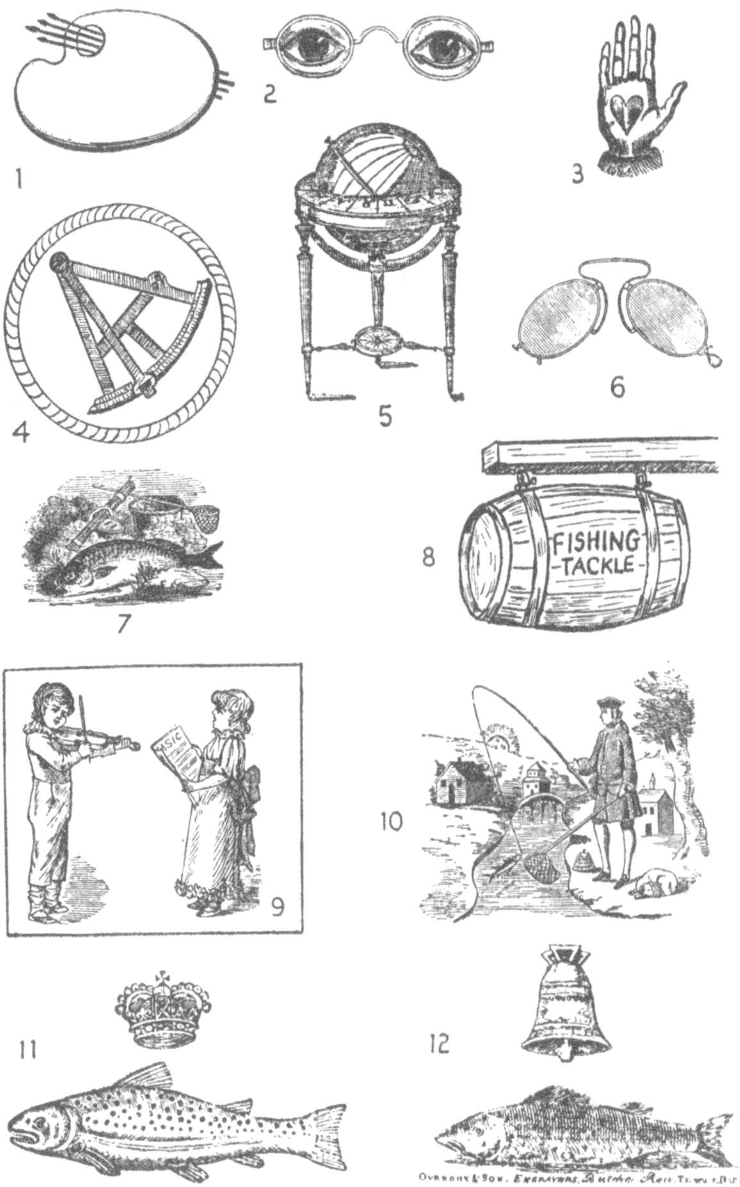

ARTISTS AND OPTICIANS.

1. The Golden Palette.
2. Optician's Sign.
3. Heart and Hand.
4. The Quadrant.
5. The Globe.
6. Optician's Sign.
7. Victorian Tackle Dealer.
8. Modern Cornish Sign.
9. Victorian Music Teacher.
10. Compleat Angler.
11. Fish and Crown, London, 1818.
12. Bell and Fish, London, 1803.

be made of the Golden Fly of Hardys' of George Street, Edinburgh.

The Gunsmiths, whose principal sign was the Crossed Guns, took this from the arms of the Company of Gunsmiths. These are blazoned: 'Argent, two guns in saltire proper, in chief the letter G, in base the letter Y, sable, each crowned with a regal crown; on the dexter side, in fesse, a barrel; and on the sinister, three balls all of the second.'

Other signs are known, such as the Cross Bow of Jeffery Dunn in the Haymarket (1760), the Golden Blunderbuss of Edward Bond in Lombard Street (1777), and the Ranged Deer in the Minories (1673). Many signs still remain, among them the Golden Gun of Martins of Frederick Street, Edinburgh, and the stone Stag of Darlows of Orford Hill, Norwich.

An interesting sign was the Two Swordsmen of Andrew Read of Hog Hill, Norwich, in the eighteenth century. Read conducted a school of Swordsmanship, and his sign appears to be unique.

The Music Sellers, the Musicians and the Musical Instrument Makers all used the musical instruments of the period for signs, and the following, taken from the Bagford Bills, gives us some idea of how this was done:

> 'Richard Meares, Musical Instrument Maker, is removed from Ye Golden Viol in Leaden Hall Street to ye North side of St Pauls Churchyard at Ye Golden Viol and Hautboy, where he sells all sorts of musical instruments etc.'

Many instruments were used as signs, but most commonly the Golden Harp, the Harp and Crown, the Violin, Hautboy and German Flute, the Golden Flute and the French Horn. Two interesting London signs were the Trumpett and Horne of William Bull in Castle Street (1700) and the Drum and Colours of Robert Horne of Barbican (1796).

Orpheus or Orpheus and Lute were used as signs by instrument makers, and Novello, the Music Publisher, carried on his business at the Golden Crotchet, while Jonathan Woolls, Musician, had the Tabor and Pipe in the Strand (1749).

The arms of the Musicians' Society (incorporated 1604) are blazoned: 'Azure, a swan with wings expanded argent within a double tressure flory counterflory or, on a chief gules a pale between two lions passant guardant of the third, thereon a rose of the fourth, seeded gold, barbed vert.' The crest is a Golden Lyre and this device was to be found as the sign of a musician.

The makers of Bows and Arrows do not appear to have made use of signs, possibly because their use had declined before the signs came into general use. The arms of their guilds are given because it is highly probable that in some cases these would have been used on signboards.

The arms of the Company of Bowyers are blazoned: 'Sable, on a chevron between three floats or, as many mullets of the first.' Crest: 'On a wreath three longbows interlaced, one erect and two in saltire, gules.'

The arms of the Company of Fletchers are blazoned: 'Azure, a chevron between three arrows or, headed and feathered argent.' The crest is 'A demi-angel proper with wings endorsed or, vested of the last, holding a bundle of arrows or.'

The arms of the Company of Longbow String Makers are blazoned: 'Azure, a hank or knot of bowstrings in pale or, on a chief argent three bows.' The crest is: 'A man vested proper shooting with a bow and arrow of the last.'

The sign of the Dial was used by the majority of the Clock Makers, and the most common variations were the Dial and Crown, the Dial and Star, the Dial and Two Crowns, as well as the Dial and Three Crowns (Alexander Cumming, New Bond Street, 1770), and the Unicorn and Dial near Strand Bridge (1711). The arms of the Clockmakers' Company were also used as a sign and are blazoned: 'Sable, a clock, the four pillars thereof erected on four lions, and on each capital a globe with a cross, and in the midst an imperial crown, all or.' The supporters are Father Time with his scythe and a crowned Emperor with his sceptre. It was the presence of the Crown as a charge in the arms that led to its widespread use on the signboards.

The Clock and Watch Makers today use a far more practical sign than our ancestors, for they provide public clocks which serve the dual purpose; for instance the well-known clock of Benson of Ludgate Hill or the hundreds of H. Samuel clocks scattered throughout the country.

The Instrument Makers used signs according to the various branches of their trade; for instance the Optical Instrument Makers and Opticians had the Spectacles, or Archimedes or combinations of both. The usual styles were the Golden Spectacles, Archimedes' Head or Archimedes and the Three Spectacles.

Archimedes, ancient Greek physicist and geometrician, was born in Syracuse about 287 and is said to have set fire to the Roman Fleet at the siege of Syracuse by means of magnifying or burning glasses. The sign of the Three Spectacles is taken from the arms of the Spectacle Makers' Company which are blazoned: 'Argent, three pairs of spectacles vert, garnished or.'

In Victorian times opticians had giant pairs of Golden Spectacles above their shops, in many cases the frames contained eyes, and in later years these could be lit by interior electric lamps. Opticians no longer use these signs but in their windows may be seen small glass plaques bearing the arms of the Spectacle Makers' Company, the present shield having two pairs of spectacles, a globe and a pair of dividers.

James Ferguson's Head was the sign of an Optical Instrument Maker in New Bond Street (1780), chosen because Ferguson (1710–1776), who was a Fellow of the Royal Society, was a prominent scientific lecturer. The custom of choosing prominent people as the subject of signboards was quite general, for example, Samuel Scatliff, Optician of Cornhill (1750) at Friar Bacon's Head, Henry Shuttleworth of Ludgate Street (1795) at Sir Isaac Newton's Head, and Dudley Adams of Fleet Street (1790) at Tycho Brahe's Head.

Tycho Brahe was a celebrated Danish astronomer (1546–1601), a fellow worker of Johann Kepler (1571–1630), famous for his discoveries concerning the motions of the planets.

The Chirurgical Instrument Makers used representations of the instruments for their signs, such as lancets, scalpels and trepans, and Samuel Glover on London Bridge in the seventeenth century traded at the Sceptre and Heart.

The Scientific Instrument Makers had a wide variety of signs using instruments, the most common being the Quadrant, the Globe and Quadrant, the Globe, the Orrery, the Sphere and the Sun. Combinations of all these are known, including Hadley's Quadrant and Visual Glasses of Benjamin Martin of Fleet Street (1740) and the Globe, Quadrant and Spectacles of Thomas Ripley, Hermitage Bridge, London (1760).

Several signs incorporated the Orrery, which was a clockwork device made to show the movements of the planets, named after Charles Boyle, Earl of Orrery, for whom one of these instruments was made.

In 1705 Thomas Tax, Instrument Maker, traded at the Halbert and Hart, 81, Lombard Street, formerly known as the Saw (presumably another instrument maker), and George Cooke of the same trade had the Saw and Crown at 82, Lombard Street.

The Hand and Hammer was the sign of the Gold Beaters, a highly skilled trade, though always numerically small. Gold Leaf, that commodity so much in demand by the sign-painters and gilders, was beaten out by hand, and even today its method of manufacture differs little from that of a few centuries ago.

The Engravers, to whom we owe so much for their work on the billheads and trade-cards of the tradesmen, had a variety of signs without any special bearing on their craft. Their traditional sign was the Golden Head, widely used, though a high proportion of engravers had no sign at all.

Naturally enough all the Scale Makers had a pair of Scales as a sign, generally appearing as the Hand and Scales, the Angel and Scales, the Heart and Scales, and Justice and Scales. The blindfold figure of Justice with the Scales was quite popular, and with some of the Angel and Scales signs the eyes were unbandaged.

Many of these old scalemakers' signs survive; in Norwich, for instance, Bentalls (formerly Wests) in Exchange Street have preserved the figure of Justice by mounting it on a plinth inside the shop.

Larwood and Hotten record the sign of the Angel and Stillyards, though it was the sign of a Soap Maker, but on some of the signboards the steelyard is shown above the figure holding the pair of scales (the steelyard being a balance arm with a sliding weight).

In the history of the National Provincial Bank by Aytoun Ellis, under the title *Bold Adventure*, mention is made of a pair of scales; that is to say a balance or a beam made in 1761 by Samuel Read at the sign of the Angel and King's Arms in Aldersgate. The balance still exists at Prescott's Office branch in London.

The Little Wooden Midshipman, sign of the trade of Nautical Instrument Maker, received much prominence in Dickens' story of *Dombey and Son*. In Chapter IV we read:

'Anywhere in the immediate vicinity there might be seen outfitting warehouses ready to pack off anybody anywhere, fully equipped in half an hour; and little timber midshipmen in obsolete naval uniforms, eternally employed outside the shops of nautical instrument makers in taking observations of the hackney coaches. One of these effigies which might be called, familiarly, the woodenest—of that which thrust itself out above the pavement, right leg foremost, with a suavity the least endurable, and had the shoe buckles and flapped waistcoat the least reconcilable to human reason, and bore at its right eye the most offensively disproportionate piece of machinery.'

As was the custom with all of these small figures, they were taken into the shop at night for safety and replaced first thing in the morning when the shutters were removed, and Dickens mentions this in the story.

In his notes on 'Edinburgh Shop Signs' in the *Edinburgh Evening News* of May 6, 1950, A. N. R. writes:

'There is a splendid sailor of olden times at the shop of David Stalker, in Commercial Street, Leith. He wears a two cornered hat, and a dark blue gold-braided and gold-epauletted tailcoat. His golden-handled sword hangs by his left side, and he is looking through a sextant with his right eye. He is the finest and handsomest shop sign in Edinburgh.'

XI

BOOKSELLERS AND PUBLISHERS

Booksellers, Printsellers, Publishers, Stationers, Circulating Libraries

MANY of the early Stationers used the arms of the Stationers' Company as a sign, and on the token of Samuel Williams of Lincoln (1667) these arms are shown. The arms are blazoned: 'Azure, on a chevron or, between three Bibles lying fesseways gules, garnished, leaved, and clasped of the second (clasps downwards), an eagle rising proper enclosed by two roses gules, seeded or, barbed vert; from the top of the chief a demi-circle of glory edged with clouds proper, therein a dove displayed argent; over the head a circle of the last.' The crest is an open Bible.

It is from these arms that the most common of the Stationers' signs were taken. The Bible, the Hand and Bible, the Dove, the Bible and Dove, the Eagle or Spread Eagle, and the Bible and Crown.

William Fenner in Paternoster Row (1760) had the Angel and Bible, Arthur Lyon in Threadneedle Street (1750) traded at the Ink Bottle, and Benjamin Moore in Newgate Street (1758) had the Paper Mill.

Many of the old businesses are still in existence such as Lepard and Smith, which in 1757 was owned by William Lepard at the Hand and Bible, Tooley Street,

Southwark; and Cooper, Dennison and Walkden of St Bride Street who have descended from Richard Walkden at the sign of the Bell on London Bridge (1735).

In 1682 a Stationer in St Martin's Lane used the sign of the Royal Hand and Globe, William Weeks of Plymouth (1659) had a Clasped Book on his token, John Williams of Plymouth (1659) has an Open Book on his token (probably the Bible from the crest of the Stationers), and Christopher Coningsby in Fleet Street (1692) had the Golden Turk's Head.

John Trudgill, Ballad Printer, in the Barbican (seventeenth century), used the sign of the Nobody; Thomas Kaygill, Print Seller, Drury Lane (1760) worked at the sign of the Laughing Painter; and Anthony Solemne, Printer of Norwich (1584) had the White Dove.

The Print Sellers, by and large, had similar signs to the Booksellers, principally the Golden Head, or the head of a famous artist such as Rembrandt or Hogarth. In the same manner, the Circulating Libraries, which were established about the middle of the eighteenth century, had such signs as Dryden's Head, Otway's Head and Pope's Head.

The Booksellers as a class produced more variety of signs and signboards than any other group of traders; their choice ranged far and wide, but they can be grouped roughly in four sections. These are (1) Birds and Animals, (2) Religious Objects and Themes, (3) Heads of Famous People and (4) Miscellaneous Charges.

Among the Birds, Animals and Fishes the following are typical examples:

The Three Herrings (1675), Dolphin (1699), Falcon (1612), Pigeon (1698), Black Raven (1711), Black Spread Eagle (1659), Cat and Parrot (1612), Hedgehog (1555), Tiger's Head (1588) and the White Greyhound (1600).

Among the Religious Objects and Themes used by Booksellers on their signboards the following give an idea of their variety, and these come mainly from the sixteenth century:

Our Lady of Pity (1542), The Resurrection (1580), Holy Ghost (1558), Trinity (1520), St Augustine (1560), St Paul's Head (1640) and Brazen Serpent (1544).

Naturally enough the Bible figured largely on the signs in combination with such devices as Hand (1691), Anchor (1742), Peacock (1688), Lamp (1759), Key (1761), Ball (1761), Dove (1718), Sun, and the Three Legs (1699). It was also used as the Three Bibles (1650), Hanging Bible (1760), Blue Bible (1632) and the Heart and Bible (1667).

The Bible and Crown was used by John and James Rivington of Paternoster Row in 1753; the House of Rivington dates back to 1688, and is carried on today in King Street, W.C.2. The Bible and Crown is still used by B. T. Batsford's, and Sir Ambrose Heal's book *The Signboards of Old London Shops* bears the imprint 'At the Sign of the Bible and Crown, Mayfair, London.' The connection is traced back to Robert Peake, the Bible and Crown, Snow Hill (1611) and H. Piers, the Bible and Fan, later the Bible and Crown, in Holborn (1742). The Bible and Crown was widely used in the provinces by Booksellers as well as the Victorian version of the Bible, Sceptre and Crown.

A famous Bookseller of the eighteenth century, Robert Dodsley in Pall Mall, traded at the sign of Tully's Head and these verses were written about it:

'Where Tully's bust and honour'd name
Point out the venal page,
There Dodsley consecrates to fame
The classics of his age:
Persist to grace this humble post,
Be Tully's Head the sign,
Till future booksellers shall boast
To sell their tomes at thine.'

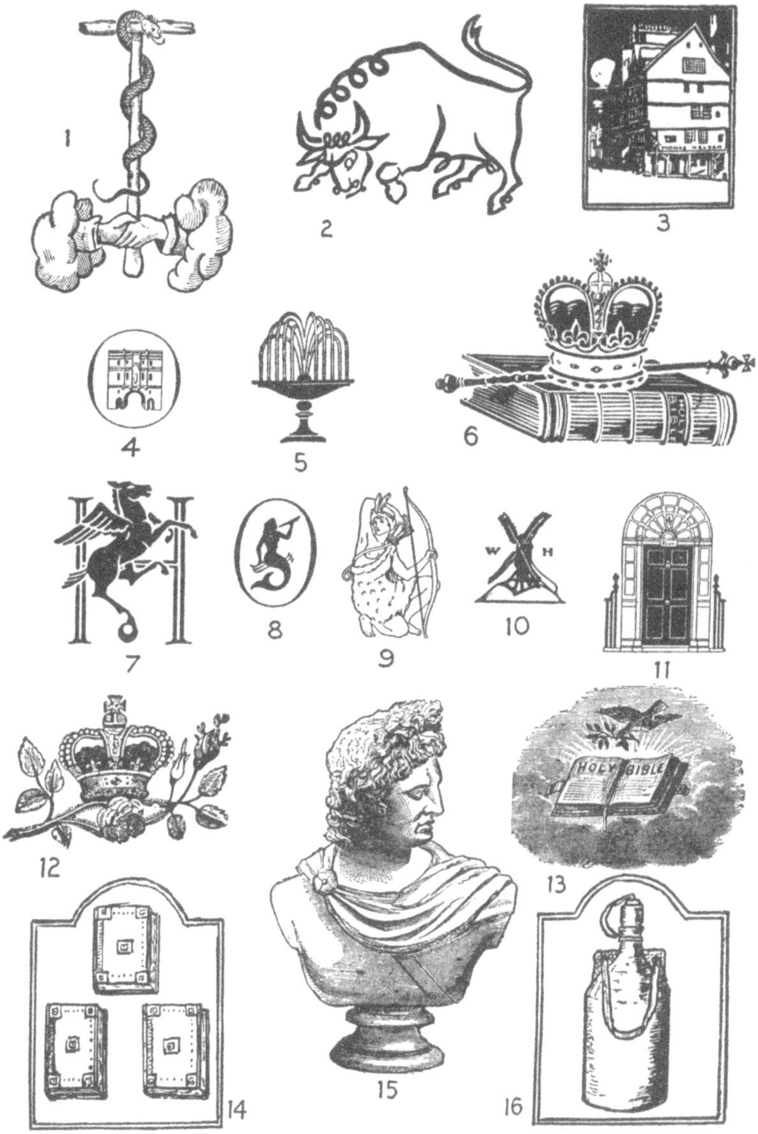

BOOKSELLERS AND PUBLISHERS

1. The Brazen Serpent.
2. Hutchinson.
3. Nelson.
4. Routledge and Kegan Paul.
5. Collins.
6. The Bible, Crown and Sceptre.
7. Harrap.
8. Michael Joseph.
9. Cassell.
10. Heinemann.
16. The Ink Bottle.
11. Batsford.
12. Rose and Crown.
13. The Bible and Dove.
14. The Three Bibles.
15. Apollo's Head

The following list of Heads gives some indication of the variety used by Booksellers and it is safe to say that every one, however small, boasted of a sign, and it was generally a Head:

Lord Bacon (1735), Locke (1718), Homer (1735), Horace (1720), Seneca (1711), Jonson (1655), Milton (1759), Dryden (1761), Pope (1735), Addison (1740), Sterne (1795), Garrick (1768), Shakespeare (1760), Erasmus (1700), Otway (1754) and Hogarth (1755).

Among the miscellaneous signs of Booksellers are many devices not associated with their trade, such as the Gun of Thomas Ewster, Ivy Lane (1649), which sign was used by a number of booksellers for no apparent reason. Other signs included the Three Arrows (1556), Sampson and Lyon (1700), Blue Anchor (1675), Trunk (1684), Helmet (1550), Golden Frying Pan (1680) and the Bell (1695).

The Looking Glass of J. Blare, London Bridge (1688) took its origin from the word speculum which was, in the Middle Ages, a common name for certain classes of books. The title of the *Daily Mirror* newspaper of today illustrates this point.

The Ship and Black Swan was the sign of Thomas Longman, Paternoster Row (1725), and this business has been carried on in the name of Longman, Green since 1859. Finally, the business of William Sandby, without Temple Bar (1765), whose sign was the Ship, was sold in 1768 to John Murray, under which name it is still carried on in Albemarle Street.

Mention should be made of the colophon of the publishers, formerly an inscription or device placed at the end of the book containing the title, printer's name and date and place of printing. This has survived in the use of a distinctive device on the title page, such as the Lud Gate of Routledge and Kegan Paul which appears at the front of this book. Other examples include the Ship and Dial of Harraps, the Belle Sauvage of Cassells, the Door of Batsfords, the Fountain of Collins, the Windmill of Heinemann and the Mermaid of Michael Joseph.

XII

BANKERS AND GOLDSMITHS

Bankers, Goldsmiths, Jewellers, Pawnbrokers, Silversmiths

THE Jewellers in their choice of signs usually made the Pearl an essential component. In eighteenth-century London there were the Crown and Pearl and the Ring and Pearl, and in Norwich, Dunham and Yallop traded at the Eagle and Pearl. This latter sign, bearing the date 1769, is preserved in the Strangers' Hall Museum there.

Leroy of St James's Street in the seventeenth century made an interesting choice, the Pearl of Venice. The Ring often appeared on Jewellers' signs and in Old Lombard Street there were both the Anchor and Ring and the Unicorn and Ring.

In *The Signboards of Old London Shops* Heal records several examples of the use of the Pearl and the Ring under the heading of Goldsmiths. The trade of Goldsmith was so closely linked with that of the Jeweller and Silversmith that it is difficult to place these signs under separate headings, and it may be safer to group them all together.

The list includes Thomas Chesson of Cheapside in 1736, at the Unicorn and Pearl; Forster and Johnson of

Wood Street in 1760 at the Pearl: George Pinnock of High Holborn in 1760 at the Star and Pearl, and Paul Wright of Foster Lane in 1771 at the Parrot and Pearl.

Among those using the Ring were the Star and Ring of John Robinson of New Bond Street in 1759, the Hand, Ring and Crown of Elizabeth Godfrey of Norris Street in 1760 and the Gold Ring of Basil Denn, Jnr. on London Bridge in 1743.

Signs peculiar to the Goldsmiths were based frequently on examples of their craft such as the Golden Ewer, the Golden Vase, the Golden Cup and the Golden Urn. The Goldsmiths who became Goldsmith Bankers are presumed to have taken the word Banker in the time of Charles I from the Italian word *banco* meaning a heap or pile, in this case, of money.

They started by lending surplus funds to merchants at rates of interest, and for money deposited with them they issued receipts, called Goldsmiths' Notes, the first kind of Bank Note in England. In the *Little Directory of London* in 1667, there may be found a list of 'Keepers of the running cashes' who were goldsmiths carrying out the early duties of banking.

The sign of the Cup was taken from the arms of the Goldsmiths' Company which are blazoned: 'Quarterly gules and azure, in the first and fourth a leopard's head or; in the second and third a covered cup, and in chief two round buckles, the tongues fesseways, points to the dexter, all of the third.' The crest is a demi-lady holding a pair of scales and a touchstone, and the supporters are two unicorns.

Martins Bank, whose Head Office is in Liverpool, display a sign which is a combination of two Banking Houses —Martins of Lombard Street and the Bank of Liverpool. This sign is a shield bearing a Liver Bird, on a chief a Grasshopper, the latter charge being the sign of Martins of London.

The Grasshopper is taken from the crest of Sir Thomas Gresham, the famous Elizabethan merchant, founder of the Royal Exchange, and reference to this will be found on page 27 in the chapters devoted to Grocers' signs. Sir Thomas Martin, Lord Mayor of London in 1589, was apprenticed to Gresham, and it is believed that he took over the business of Goldsmith when the latter died. However, the Grasshopper hung over the premises at 68, Old Lombard Street as far back as 1563 and records show that Charles Duncombe and Richard Kent were there in 1672.

In 1688 it was Richard Smith, in 1699 Stone and Martin, in 1712 Martin, and in 1769 Martin, Stone, all of whom in turn used the Grasshopper as their sign. The original Grasshopper, made of copper, was stolen in the rebuilding of 1800, but a faithful copy was made and hung outside the new building. Replicas of the Grasshopper may be seen outside many of the branches in the south of the country.

The Bank of Liverpool, established in 1831, incorporated in 1882, amalgamated with Martins in 1918 under the name of the Bank of Liverpool and Martins and this was shortened to the present title in 1928. The Bank of Liverpool must be regarded as the principal in the amalgamation, and for this reason no doubt the principal charge is the Liver Bird, taken from the arms of the City of Liverpool. The name of the bird was coined from the word Liverpool, for it was originally intended for the eagle of St John the Evangelist.

The arms of the Westminster Bank, which were granted on May 22, 1928, appear as a sign outside the many branches and the blazon runs: 'Azure, semee of roses argent, barbed and seeded proper, a fesse wavy also argent, in the quarter a portcullis or'. The History of the Bank makes no mention of any signs used by the earlier houses,

BANKERS AND GOLDSMITHS.

1. Lloyds. 3. Midland. 5. Martins.
2. Westminster. 4. Barclays. 6. National Provincial.

for though the London and Westminster Bank was founded in 1834 it can be traced back to Hankey of 1685 who merged with Consolidated in 1863. They merged in turn with Parrs in 1896 and London County and Westminster in 1918. Another link with the early days is that of Crompton, Newton of Derby, established in 1685, merged in Crompton and Evans Union Bank in 1877, and finally with Parrs in 1914.

One of the earliest of the Lombard Street Goldsmiths and Bankers to have a sign was Thomas Muschamp, Goldsmith to Queen Elizabeth in 1560, and he conducted his business at the Ring and Ruby.

The Golden Fleece, familiar sign for the woollen trade, was also the sign of a well-known seventeenth-century Goldsmith Banker named Bernard Turner of Lombard Street. The Unicorn of Lombard Street was the sign of one of the most famous and wealthy of all the early bankers, Alderman Edward Backwell. He was the private banker to Charles II, the East India Company, and State banker to the Commonwealth.

Backwell kept accounts of most of the famous merchants and personalities of his day, and from one of his ledgers we learn that the receipts of the East India Company for the year ending March 25, 1671 amounted to £237,900, a colossal sum of money in those days. He acted as a clearing house, all the bankers of the period had accounts with him and many of his ledgers still survive. They are in the possession of Messrs. Child (now Glyn Mills), for Backwell's grandson married the daughter of Sir Francis Child (1642–1713) and their sons, William and Barnaby, became partners in the banking house of Child.

The mention of Sir Francis Child recalls his well-known sign Ye Marigold. The sign of Ye Marigold indicated the bank mentioned by Charles Dickens in his *Tale of Two Cities* under the name of Tellsons.

'Tellsons Bank by Temple Bar was an old-fashioned place, even in the year one thousand seven hundred and eighty. It was very small, very dark, very ugly, very incommodious. . . Your money came out of, or went into, wormy old wooden drawers, particles of which flew up your nose and down your throat when they were opened and shut.'

This famous old bank is now known as Childs Branch of Glyn Mills, by whom they were absorbed in 1923.

Lloyds Bank, upon whose cheques appear the familiar Black Horse and the date 1677, trace this sign back to the Goldsmith Stokes, a friend of Pepys, at 53, Lombard Street. John Bland followed Stokes and his son moved the sign to 62, Lombard Street, at the corner of Birchin Lane. This eventually became Barnett, Hoares, who were incorporated in the business of Lloyds. The title then became Lloyds, Barnetts and Bosanquets Bank, subsequently shortened to Lloyds Bank.

Jeremiah Snow, the famous Cromwellian and Post-Restoration Goldsmith and Banker, conducted his business at the Golden Anchor. At the time of the South Sea Crisis, Gay wrote the following lines about Thomas Snow, Banker of the Golden Anchor, and they indicate the esteem in which Snow was held:

'When credit sank and commerce gasping lay,
Thou stood'st; nor sent'st one bill unpaid away,
When not a guinea clinked on Martin's boards,
And Atwell's self was drained of all his hoards,
Thou stood'st (an Indian King in size and hue)
Thy unexhausted shop was our Peru.'

The bank later passed to Strahan, Paul, who became bankrupt in 1855. In the same year the London and Westminster Bank opened a Temple Bar branch (after closing of Strahan, Paul and Bates) nearby and employed many of the old staff, but they did not take over the bankrupt business and are thus not in a position to claim the Golden Anchor.

The Golden Bottle of Hoare's Bank was the sign of John Hoare, Goldsmith and Banker in Cheapside in Elizabethan times. The earliest surviving ledger goes back as far as 1673. Hoare's were to be found in Fleet Street where today at No. 37 the sign of the Golden Bottle may still be seen and this device still appears on the cheques of this ancient Banking House.

The sign of the Midland Bank which appears on their cheques and brochures, though not outside on a sign-board, is a coat of arms granted as late as 1952, though its origin goes back to 1889. The blazon reads 'Quarterly 1st and 4th azure, a blend of lozenges conjoined or, 2nd and 3rd per pale indented of the last and gules, over all a cross also gules thereon in chief a sword erect proper, hilt and pommel of the second and in fesse a mural crown between four ermine spots, gold.'

The crest is a dragon's wing issuing from a mural crown and the supporters are a dragon and griffin. The arms bear symbols corresponding to those on the arms of the Cities of London and Birmingham: the red cross and the sword from London and the quarterings, crown and ermine from Birmingham.

The Midland Bank, formerly the London Joint City and Midland Bank, was founded in Birmingham in 1836, though in the various amalgamations that took place several older banks were included. Among these earlier banks were W. B. Collis of Stourbridge (1762–1770), Little and Woodcock of Coventry (1762–1865), Wright of London (1759–1840) and Banc y Llong of Aberystwyth (1762–1815).

It is through Wright, acquired in 1840 by the London Joint Stock Bank, that the ancestry can be traced back to the goldsmith banking days. William Wright, Goldsmith, had his business in Great Russell Street in 1669 and his son Anthony who succeeded him is known to have had an extensive banking business at the sign of

BANKERS AND GOLDSMITHS.

1. At the Sign of the Eagle and Pearl, Norwich.
2. Golden Cup.
3. Marygold, Child's Bank, Fleet Street.
4. Star and Pearl.
5. Golden Urn.
6. Pawnbrokers' Sign.
7. Crown, Ring and Pearl.

Ye Golden Cup, Common Garden, in 1759. Soon after this it was moved to Henrietta Street, Covent Garden, where under the name of Wright it remained until 1840.

Though the Midland Bank today use their grant of arms as a sign, at least on the cheques, they could if they wished lay claim to the ancient sign of the Goldsmith Wright, Ye Golden Cup, a favourite sign for a Goldsmith.

Ye Three Squirrels was one of the ancient banking signs and can be traced back to Henry Pinckney, Goldsmith, 'over against St Dunstan's Church in Fleet Street' in 1649. The date of establishment is not known but it goes back possibly to the early days of the seventeenth century. In Pepys' *Diary* under the date of December 1, 1660 we read that 'Mr Stepney and I sent into London and calling on Mr Pinckney the Goldsmith he took us to the Tavern and gave us a pint of wine'.

Henry Pinckney was joined later by his brother William from the Golden Dragon at Inner Temple Gate, and in 1720 Richard Nicholls came into the business from the Golden Key. In 1754 the title of the bank as it had become was Gosling, Bennet and Gosling, and in 1794 it was known as Gosling and Sharpe, a title which remained for 102 years until the amalgamation with Barclays in 1896.

The Three Anchors of Lombard Street was the sign of John Freame, Goldsmith, prior to 1694, and in 1698 the business known as Freame and Gould. The Three Anchors remained until 1728 when John Freame bought the Black Spread Eagle at 56, Lombard Street from a Scrivener and moved his business to the new premises. The Black Spread Eagle had been a Goldsmith's shop prior to its acquisition by Currier the Scrivener; the earliest known occupants were James Taylor, Goldsmith in 1676 and Jeremiah Marlow, Goldsmith in 1694.

The Black Spread Eagle, now known as the sign of Barclays Bank, has been used by them continuously from the days of Freame. In 1759 it was Freame, Barclay and Freame, in 1770 Freame, Smith, Bevan and Bening, and in 1776 they were Barclay, Bevan and Bening.

In 1791 the title was Barclay and Tritton, and in 1888 the name was the long one of Barclay, Bevan, Tritton, Ransom, Bouverie and Company. In 1896 the great amalgamation of twenty banks took place under the name of Barclay, the three major members being Barclay of London, Gurney of Norwich and Jonathan Backhouse of Darlington. It was in this amalgamation that the famous Three Squirrels of Gosling and Sharpe was acquired. The present title is Barclays Bank which dates from 1917, and today Barclays' cheques still bear the Black Spread Eagle and the sign appears outside many of the branches.

The blazoning of the Spread Eagle is 'Argent, an Eagle displayed sable charged on the body and on each wing with a Ducal coronet of the field.' The addition of the Three Crowns to the Black Spread Eagle in 1937 provides an interesting link with the past, for the Three Crowns was another of the Lombard Street signs, from No. 43, at least as early as 1667.

It is on this site that the Head Office of Barclays Bank (Dominion, Colonial and Overseas) may be found; thus the union of the Eagle with the Three Crowns symbolises the union of the Bank with its largest affiliation. An unusual use of the sign may be seen in Norwich at the Orford Place branch where the new oaken doors have bronze knockers in the form of the Black Spread Eagle.

The National Provincial Bank displays an heraldic shield on its cheques and publications, but this does not appear outside the branches as a sign. The arms, granted in 1952, are blazoned: 'Per chevron azure bezantee or, in base a representation of the Bishop's Gate anciently in the City of London ensigned with an urn supported by two squirrels all in stonework proper'. The arms make a rebus of the address of Head Office which is at 15, Bishopsgate: fifteen Bezants above the replica of Bishop's Gate.

The squirrels denote thrift and foresight and the urn represents a flower pot, for the City Office was built on the site of the Flower Pot Inn. The Bishop's Gate was an ancient landmark and in the thirteenth century its maintenance and defence were in the hands of the German Merchants of the Steel Yard, members of the Hanseatic League. The gate remained until 1731 when it was taken down, and the last gate on the site was built in 1735 and removed in 1760.

The National Provincial Bank was founded in 1833 but by its amalgamation with the Union and Smiths Bank in 1918 it can trace its history back to 1668 in the person of Thomas Smith, Draper and Banker of Nottingham, later Smith and Payne of Lombard Street.

Other old-established banks that were included in the various amalgamations were Tugwell of Bath (1760), Dover Bank (about 1700), Pretor of Sherborne (1750) and Miles, Cave and Baillie of Bristol (1750). The existing records do not show any of these banks as having used a sign though of course it is possible.

In 1920 the National Provincial purchased the capital of Coutts, an old established firm of Bankers with aristocratic connections, who trace their history back to George Middleton, Goldsmith, of St Martin's Lane in 1692.

The sign of a Pawnbroker, that of the Three Golden Balls, must surely be the most familiar of all the trade signs. With changing social conditions, the pawnbroker himself has become something of a rarity, and the signs are becoming fewer. In Norwich, the sole remaining pawnbroker, Boston of Orford Street, as if in defiance, sports two sets of Golden Balls, one above the other.

These signs were originally blue; they appear to have come into use as the Golden Balls in the early part of the nineteenth century. The generally accepted origin of the Three Balls is that the Lombard Merchants, the early pawnbrokers, took these from the arms of the Dukes of Medici. The arms were five bezants azure, the bezant being the heraldic flat golden disc or roundel supposed to be derived from the gold coins of Byzantium found by the Crusaders.

These bezants appear on the badge of the Midland Bank, in the form of a circle which surrounds a golden griffin, the traditional guardian of treasure. The shield of the National Provincial Bank also bears the golden bezants.

It is interesting to note that the Pawnbroker's sign always had Three Golden Balls, never less, never more, though the Mercers used the single Golden Ball and a seventeenth-century music house in Bow Street displayed Two Golden Balls.

In Lombard Street itself, no sign of Three Balls can be traced, but at No. 49 in 1667 John Thrusby kept running cashes at the sign of The Ball. The sign later passed to a hatter, who changed it to the Golden Ball, a name it kept as late as 1765. One pawnbroker used a sign which belonged to the Grocery trade, the Sugarloaf; 'Thomas Seth at the Sugarloaf in Fore Street, Pawnbroker' in the year 1711.

XIII

INSURANCE AND BUILDING SOCIETIES

Insurance Societies, Building Societies

THE Insurance Companies make wide use of signs or emblems, not only on exterior signboards but on policies, notepaper, prospectuses and proposal forms. Many of these signs are by constant repetition so familiar that the name of the company is unnecessary to identify the office.

The majority are based on the coats of arms of the companies, generally a simplified form to make identification easy, or else the use of one or more of the principal charges. In some cases the sign is a trade-mark taken from a prominent building, person or place associated with the title or origin of the company.

The first use of a fire insurance sign or badge was about 1680 by the Fire Office, an association founded by Dr Nicholas Barbon in 1667. The sign adopted was the Phoenix rising from the flames and a charter was granted by James II in 1688 and the title of the Phenix Office was adopted in 1705. There is no definite knowledge as to the end of this venture but it closed down some time after 1712.

The second office was the Mutual Fire Insurance, a corporation scheme founded in 1681 and abandoned in 1683. This was followed by the Friendly Society of 1683 whose badge was the Hale Crest taken from its founder and this society lasted until 1781. The fourth in order of foundation, the General Insurance, about 1681–1700, left no records, but the fifth, the Hand-in-Hand, founded in 1696 as 'Contributors for insuring Houses, Chambers or Rooms from Loss by Fire, by Amicable Contribution' is famous for its clasped hands sign.

The early Fire Offices maintained their own fire engines which were manned by Watermen dressed in the distinctive livery of their office. As the houses were not numbered and streets not always named distinctly, Fire Marks or distinctive badges were necessary for identification purposes. It should be noted that as the Watermen were paid for their attendance at all fires, whether the buildings were insured by their company or not, they co-operated in putting out fires wherever they could find them.

The details of the signs and badges of a few of the leading companies are given in chronological order of their foundation.

The familiar emblem of the Sun is used by the Sun Insurance Office, which is the oldest insurance office in the world trading in its own name, and was founded in April, 1710. The origins of the company can be traced back to 1706 when Charles Povey founded the Exchange House Fire Office for Town, which in 1708 issued a Sun Fire Mark. The business was taken over by the company of London Insurers in 1709 and in 1710 the Sun Fire Office was launched. The Head Office is at 63, Threadneedle Street, E.C.2, and their device is blazoned: 'The sun in his splendour, with a human face on its disc and environed with rays, alternately straight and wavy'.

The Westminster Fire Office, whose sign is the Portcullis and Feathers, was founded in 1717 at Tom's Coffee

House in St Martin's Lane. The badge was adopted on September 3, 1717, from a design of Roger Askew, a Director. The Portcullis was taken from the arms of the City of Westminster, and the Feathers out of compliment to the Prince of Wales (afterwards George II). The Prince had already shown his interest in keeping down the ravages of fire, in particular in actually assisting at the fire in the French Chapel and Library in Spring Gardens in 1716, and it is certain that he was favourably disposed towards the Westminster because, through his agent, he insured six of his properties with them during their first year. The first Fire Marks were of cast lead which was used for nearly a hundred years, and were generally serially numbered, followed by thin copper plates which were not numbered. The Head Office of the Westminster is 27–28, King Street, Covent Garden, W.C.2.

The emblem largely used by the Royal Exchange Assurance is a representation of the Exchange building itself. The foundation date is 1720 but the origin of the office can be traced back to the Public Assurance Office of Mr Case Billingsley of 1717. When Billingsley's application for a charter was refused he and his associates bought up an old charter of the Mines Royal, Mineral and Battery works and for a while transacted marine insurance under it. A Grant of Arms was made in 1721 and restated in 1905 thus: 'Azure, on a Hill the Royal Exchange, both proper, the last adorned with Gold, in chief two shipps the dexter under sail, the hull or, masts sails and rigging proper, the sinister ship riding at anchor with the sails furl'd emblazon'd as before, and for the crest a demy angell proper cloathed with a crimson garment, girdle of the same, wings displayed or, in his right hand the sun, in his left a crescent and crowned with a ducal coronet, the North Starr issuing out of it or, supported on the dexter side by a Neptune proper crown'd

INSURANCE

1. Sun
2. Union Marine and General
3. Licenses and General
4. London
5. Assurance
6. Canada

7 and 8 Alliance

with an Eastern crown gold, a mantle carelessly flung over his body purpure, in his right hand a trident erect or staff proper; on the sinister by a seaman proper, shirt chequered, vestment blew lined, britches and stockins white, shoes black buckl'd silver, cap on his head blew turned up white, holding with his left hand an anchor, gold cable proper, with this motto: Trade and Navigation'.

The London Assurance founded in 1720 arose out of two marine insurance schemes, Ram's and Colebrooke's of 1719. The charter of 1720 was for marine insurance only and in 1721 a charter was obtained for fire and life. The original arms, used for many years, were altered slightly when a Grant of Arms was obtained in 1937. The shield is used on stationery, signs, flags, reports, etc., and consists of the arms of the City of London with the red cross cottised and two daggers instead of a single sword and on a chief, three anchors. The crest of Britannia and the supporters Neptune and Apollo are omitted from the everyday emblem to achieve a bold and simple device. The Head Office is at 1, King William Street, E.C.4.

The Phœnix rising from the flames is the sign of the Phœnix Assurance Company, who were established in 1782 by the sugar refiners or bakers of London, and though they had at first some hesitation in adopting the Phœnix as its name, it has always used the Phœnix as its device or badge. On January 10, 1782, the name 'The New Fire Office Company' was adopted. A little later a motion that the company be called the 'Phœnix Assurance Company' 'past in ye negative' and the name 'The Lombard Street Insurance Company for Fire' was chosen. The matter was again considered in 1783 when the name 'Ye New Fire Office or Phœnix Society' was adopted, and in 1785 it was altered to 'The Phœnix Assurance Company or New Fire Office in London'. On

January 21, 1782 the directors decided 'that the device for this Society be a shield upon an Arm with a Phœnix thereon, the inscription the word Protection with the words New Fire Office Company, London, 1782'. The Grant of Arms of November 9, 1936, assigned the following arms to the company: 'Azure, upon a billet fessewise or, inscribed "1782" in numerals sable, a Phœnix proper'. The Head Office of the Phœnix is King William Street, E.C.4.

The Norwich Union Societies by using the emblem of Norwich Cathedral have made this graceful Norman building, with its slender spire, known throughout the world. The Norwich Union Fire Insurance Society was founded in 1797 and originally used the clasped hands device on its policies and firemarks. The firemen's arm plates bore the seated figure of Justice with the clasped hands on a shield. The Norwich Union Life Assurance Society, founded in 1808, amalgamated with the Amicable in 1866, and the arms of the latter were widely used. The Amicable was granted its charter in 1706 and was the first Life Office in the world. The arms have a winged hour-glass, battlements and clasped hands encircled by a serpent. The crest is a Dove and Serpent and this was used on the fine wrought-iron gates at the entrance to Serjeants' Inn in Fleet Street. Though the cathedral is the symbol of the Societies, the Life Society still use the Amicable device and the Fire Society a shield having the castle for Norwich, St Paul's sword for London and the symbol for water, the enemy of fire.

The badge of the Thistle was used by the Caledonian, the oldest existing Scottish Insurance Company, founded by Forrest Alexander of Edinburgh in 1805. The thistle badge was used on the firemarks and in 1851 an elaborate design was introduced for the policy headings. This was a scene showing Head Office and Edinburgh Castle in the background with a figure of Caledonia, the Thistle,

Phœnix, Plough, rod of Æsculapius, Pelican, Cornucopia and a shield with the Lion of Scotland, all making a general composition.

The County Fire Office, established in 1807, has used the same basic emblem since its foundation, that of a Britannia-like figure carrying a spear instead of a trident, with seated lion and shield. The original design has a background showing a harvested field with a burning farmhouse, the central figure symbolising the protection provided by insurance against misfortune.

Atlas supporting the world is the device of the Atlas Assurance, founded in 1808, and the badge dates from the same year; it appeared on the silver armlet badge worn by the Company's firemen and on the firemarks. The birthplace of the Atlas was Will's Coffee House in Bank Buildings, where the scheme was first projected by some merchants and bankers towards the end of 1807. It is interesting to note that the Atlas agents in the Isle of Man issued both penny and halfpenny tokens in the period after the Napoleonic Wars, when there was a serious shortage of small copper coins. In the course of time there have been several minor changes in the design of the figure, the present one shows Atlas in a more secure attitude.

The North British and Mercantile Insurance Company, who were founded in 1809, have an interesting Coat of Arms granted in 1951. The crest of the figure of St Andrew indicates the Scottish origin, one supporter is a Unicorn from the arms of Lord Brand. The shield has a Castle for Edinburgh and the cross of St George for London, with a Boar's Head taken from the arms of the Duke of Gordon. Several designs had been used previously, the first dated 1809 shows the Arms of George III, the second, executed in 1837, has the Arms of Queen Victoria and both incorporate the figure of St Andrew. The third design, executed in 1879 was an elaborate

INSURANCE

1. Scottish Life.
2. Avon.
3. Railway Passengers.
4. North British.
5. Phœnix.
6. Legal & General.
7. Norwich Union Life.
8. Norwich Union.
9. Norwich Union Fire.
10. Guildhall.
11. Municipal Mutual.
12. Scottish Boiler.

pictorial scene linking Edinburgh with London and it shows two figures side by side, St Andrew and St George. The fourth design is the forerunner of the present arms and resembles a seal which bears the Arms of Edinburgh and London.

The Scottish Union and National Insurance Company who were founded in 1824 have a Grant of Arms dated 1918. Prior to this, arms were used which represented the amalgamation of the Scottish Union and Scottish National in 1878 in a form which bore a resemblance to the Royal Arms and was, for that reason, discontinued. The present shield has the saltire of St Andrew, between a Salamander for fire, two Flaming Torches representing life insurance, and an Anchor for the marine interests. A device consisting of the Thistle, Rose and Shamrock is shown on the centre of St Andrew's cross and represents the United Kingdom.

The Castle device of the Alliance Assurance Company has been in use continuously since its foundation in 1824 and today appears on all the stationery and prospectuses, as well as on exterior signboards at the branch offices. The Grant-of-Arms, dated September 4, 1933, shows the Castle on the shield supported by two lions who rest on escutcheons charged with an anchor and a rod of Aesculapius. The crest is a coronet composed of roses from which issues a flame in which are two crossed keys. The Alliance grew out of a casual meeting in the City of Sir Moses Montefiore and Nathan Rothschild.

York Minster is the emblem of the Yorkshire Insurance Company and this was adopted in 1826, two years after the foundation of the company. The device is widely used and many of the branch offices have models of York Minster on display in the windows.

The Lion of Scotland is used as an emblem by the Northern Assurance Company which was established in Aberdeen in 1836. The early firemarks and fire buckets bear the Red Lion of Scotland and the device has been in continuous use since the foundation of the Company.

The Legal and General Assurance Society, established in 1836, used the emblem of Temple Bar by reason of the fact that their offices have been situated, since 1836, a few yards east of the spot where the gateway used to stand. The crest of the Society is interesting and is blazoned: 'On a wreath of the colours a dragon rampant vert the wings edged and ribbed of the first, charged with a cross gules supporting a fasces in bend proper'. The use of the Dragon is inspired by the allegorical figure surmounting the Temple Bar memorial, the red cross represents the City of London and the fasces, the emblem of legal authority, emphasises the legal associations of the Society.

The Royal Insurance Company, established in 1845, use a plain red shield which originates with the Queen Insurance, taken over in 1891. The old Royal fire mark, taken from the crest of the Company, embodied the Liver bird, which indicates its Liverpool origin. The motto, *Tutam te sistam* (I will place thee in safety) is most appropriate and was adopted at the time of the incorporation of the Company.

The Pelican feeding its young is the badge of the Canada Life Assurance Company, established in 1847. The Pelican is the crest and the badge incorporates the beaver and maple which are symbolic of Canada.

The Prudential Assurance Company, established in 1848, use their coat-of-arms not only on their stationery and literature, but on exterior signboards as well. These are blazoned: 'Sable, three bars embattled or, two flaunches argent each charged with three martlets in pale gules'. The 'three bars embattled' are intended as an allusion to the position of the Company's premises at the ancient Holborn Bars and the six martlets are taken from the arms of Furnival, for the Offices stand on the site of

INSURANCE

1. Scottish Union and National.
2. Provincial.
3. Royal Exchange Fire Mark.
4. Bedford.
5. Federation.
6. Pearl.
7. Cornhill.
8. Westminster Fire Office.
9. Prudential.
10. Invincible.
11. Royal Exchange.

Furnival's Inn. The crest is the figure of Prudence taken from the window in New College, Oxford, which was designed by Sir Joshua Reynolds.

The Railway Passengers Assurance Company established in 1849, use as a sign the device of St George and the Dragon which was taken from the golden sovereign, and bears the legend 'the oldest accident office in the world'.

The Union Marine and General Insurance Company, established in 1863, use their crest on policies and documents, the main theme of which is Neptune sitting in his shell-chariot, harnessed to a team of sea horses. A Triton, sounding his conch accompanies him, and in the background are ships and a lighthouse. The crest is surmounted by a representation of the Liver Bird to denote the association of the Company with the City of Liverpool.

The Pearl Assurance Company, established in 1864, use a Grant-of-Arms of 1911 as their sign. The shield has a red saltire for the Borough of Holborn, in which the Head Office of the Company is situated, surmounted by the sword of St Paul from the arms of the City of London. A wounded hind also from the Borough arms refers to St Giles-in-the-Fields and the covered cup of the Goldsmiths' arms indicates St Dunstan, their patron saint, and the Borough of Stepney, where the Company had its first place of business. The crest is St Margaret of Antioch standing on the dragon from whose inside she has just emerged. Margaret was chosen because the name means a pearl and thus represents the title of the Company.

A warden in armour guarding a gateway is the emblem of the Warden Insurance Company, founded in 1875 as the Provincial Carriage Insurance Company. In 1893 the title was the Horse, Carriage and General Insurance Company and the present name and emblem were adopted in 1917.

The Scottish Boiler and General Insurance Company,

established in 1881, use a circular emblem showing a seated figure with hammer and wheel representing the engineering industry. The main business of the Company is the insurance of engineering plant and acting as consultants for installation of process plant and machinery. The figure on the emblem has as a background the saltire of St Andrew with a floral border representing Scotland and England.

The Lion of Scotland is the emblem of the Scottish Life Assurance Company who were founded in 1881. The Grant-of-Arms of 1931 reads 'Paly of six or and sable, a lion rampant gules, armed and langued azure'. The gold and black striped shield is taken from the arms of the Duke of Athol, who was the President of the Company at the time of the grant. The crest is a celestial crown of gold starred silver which also appears in the emblem as used on the stationery, etc.

The Knight in Armour, named Phronimos, meaning prudent, is the sign of the Licenses and General Insurance Company, established in 1890. The emblem appears not only on stationery and policies but outside all the branch offices as an attractive and unique sign. It was designed by the artist Walter Crane who gave it its name, and it is interesting to note that Phronimos is also the telegraphic address of the Company.

The figure of John Bunyan, a reproduction of the statue in Bedford, is the emblem of the Bedford General Insurance Company who were established in 1894. The Company was started in Bedford by eight local traders as a Mutual Plate Glass Company and the emblem of Bunyan was adopted because his statue stands opposite the first office in the town. The insurance was originally limited to Bedford but the Company grew rapidly, and in 1934 the present title was adopted, with Head Office in London and branches throughout the United Kingdom.

The Municipal Mutual Insurance, founded in 1903,

use their Coat-of-Arms on signboards as well as on their stationery. Though another device had been used earlier, the Grant-of-Arms was not made until 1950, and is blazoned: 'Or, between two swords in saltire, points upwards, a rose gules barbed and seeded proper in chief and a thistle and a daffodil both stalked and leaved also proper in fesse.' And for the crest 'upon a mural crown proper a Portcullis chained or, with a rose gules barbed and seeded also proper'. The emblems of England, Scotland and Wales indicate the area of the Company's business and the mural crown represents Local Government administration, while the portcullis is included because of its association with the City of Westminster. The Company, which is concerned with insurance for Local Authorities, was founded by thirteen Authorities in an office in Shoreditch Town Hall, and was at that time concerned only with fire risk. It is interesting to note that at the foundation meetings Councillor George Bernard Shaw represented the Borough of St Pancras.

The Provincial Insurance Company, whose head office is in Kendal, was established in 1903. The seal of the Company is used on all stationery and appears on signboards outside their Branch Offices. It is quarterly argent and gules, that is to say a quartering of white and red, and makes a sign which is easily recognised. Founded by Sir James Scott as a private venture in Bolton, the arms were those of a grant in Lorraine in 1570 to one of his ancestors. In 1919 the Head Office was moved to Kendal, where the Scott family had connections and a late-style Georgian house known as Sand Aire was purchased for this purpose.

The arms of the Cornhill Insurance Company, established in 1905, are used on exterior signboards at the Branch Offices as well as on the stationery and policies. The arms were granted in 1937 and are blazoned 'Azure, a pile reversed issuant from the base and in chief two garbs or'. The device, which is remarkably simple, consists of a golden hill and two sheaves of corn on a blue shield and is a rebus of the name of the Company.

Invincible policies, underwritten by Trafalgar Insurance Company, established in 1907, use the emblem of a battleship on all stationery, policies and advertisements. The battleship design represents H.M.S. *Invincible*, which was built in 1907 and was sister ship to the *Indomitable* and *Inflexible*. After the defeat at Coronel, the Admiralty detached the *Invincible* and *Inflexible* from the Grand Fleet and they later played a leading part in defeating the Germans at the Battle of the Falkland Islands.

The sign of the Legal Insurance Company, established in 1907, is a shield depicting the arms of each Honourable Society of the Four Inns of Court, the Inner Temple, Lincoln's Inn, Middle Temple and Gray's Inn. The first quarter bears the winged Pegasus of the Inner Temple, the second the rampant Lion of Lincoln's Inn, the third the Paschal Lamb on a red cross of the Middle Temple and the fourth the Griffin of Gray's Inn.

The Guildhall Insurance Company, established in 1919, formerly known as the Autocar Fire and Accident Insurance Company, use their coat of arms as a sign. These are blazoned: 'Sable, a terrestial globe or, on a chief of the second a Lion passant guardant of the first.' The supporters are Gog and Magog, the historic giants so long associated with the Guildhall and the civic life of London.

The Avon Insurance Company of Stratford on Avon, founded in 1925, use a white swan as a sign. The swans of the Avon are of considerable interest to Stratford's many visitors and the device was chosen because the Company's Head Office is situated there.

The Federation Mutual Insurance, formerly the National Federation of Meat Traders Mutual Insurance, incorporated in 1925, was founded over fifty years ago by a firm of Lloyds Brokers. For this reason the badge, which is a shield bearing an Ocean liner, was chosen. The ship resembles one of the Cunard giants of the old *Mauretania* days.

In common with the Banks and Insurance Companies, the Building Societies have, in the majority of cases, found it necessary to adopt individual devices or badges which appear on their stationery, advertisements, and which are used as signs. These signs are either hung outside the premises in the traditional manner or else appear on a plaque fixed outside or as a motif in the window.

The following list is a brief selection of those signs which are more commonly seen, or which have an interesting design.

The Abbey National of Baker Street, N.W.1, established in 1849, use a signboard showing a lion in a circle which bears the foundation date and the rose, thistle, shamrock and leek of the United Kingdom. Though this device appears on their stationery, all the advertisements show a man and woman, arm in arm, walking beneath a tiled umbrella, that is to say, the umbrella is in the form of a house roof. Constant repetition of this has made the 'umbrella couple' better known to the general public than the original sign of the lion.

The Alliance of Brighton, established in 1863, use the sign of the Beaver. The busy beaver with a branch in his mouth is readily understood as a symbol of house building, and the Alliance use this in several ways. Some of the branch offices have the Beaver in silhouette while others have the device on a bronze wall plaque, fixed at eye level.

The Coventry Permanent Economic, established in 1884, use a device based on the arms of Coventry showing the Elephant and Castle and Leopard. In some of the advertisements a badge incorporating the Three Spires of the city is used.

BUILDING SOCIETIES.

1. Abbey National Building Society.
2. Alliance Building Society.
3. Portman Building Society.
4. Temperance Permanent Building Society.

5–6. Coventry Permanent Economic Building Society.

7. Maidenhead Building Society.
8. Fourth City Building Society.

The Fourth City, established in 1862, use the plant called Common Thrift in flower as a badge which appears on all the advertisements, a constant reminder of the cardinal principle of the Building Society movement.

The Leeds Permanent, established in 1848, use their coat of arms on brochures and advertisements and as a sign in the branch offices' windows. The shield has a triple-towered castle and two five-pointed stars or mullets and the supporters are two owls. The crest is an owl on a mural crown holding a key. These arms are partly based on those of Leeds which have the mullets and owls. In heraldry the mullet is actually the rowel of a spur, the estoile or star has wavy points like a starfish.

The Maidenhead, established in 1859, use a five-arched bridge with the name of the society and establishment date as a badge, the design symbolises the importance of the Thames bridge to this riverside town.

The Newcastle upon Tyne Permanent, established in 1861, use the arms of Newcastle on their advertisements. The shield has three triple-towered towers, the supporters are two sea-horses and the crest is a tower with a lion holding the banner of St George.

The Portman, established in 1881, use an interesting symbol in their advertisements. It is the novelty weather house in which the man comes out for rain and the woman for fine weather. The device shows the lady out for fine, with the slogan 'for a brighter outlook'.

The Provincial, established in 1849, use their coat of arms on their pamphlets and literature, which are based on the arms of Bradford. The shield has two buglehorns and a fleece, the supporters are a ram and an owl and the crest is a castle from which a hand issues holding a key.

The Temperance Permanent, established 1854, on all their literature use the device which shows a stone arch through which may be seen a vista of home and garden. The Grant-of-Arms to the Society shows a gold archway with fountain and key; the heraldic fountain or symbol of water represents temperance. The supporters are two ermine greyhounds taken from the crest of the Shaen family, associated with the Society, and the crest is the Lion of Westminster, with a Saxon crown, the red sword of London, and a collar with three temperance fountains on the pattern of the arms of William Penn.

The Scottish Amicable, established in 1892, use a circular device which bears the name of the Society and the rampant Lion of Scotland.

XIV

MODERN SIGNS

By the end of the nineteenth century, traders' signs had almost disappeared, leaving only the Hotels, Inns and Licensed Houses to keep the custom alive. The need for pictorial representation or the display of familiar objects of trade had vanished, but, in the present century, there has been a revival of the signs.

The amazing development of proprietary brands of merchandise with its natural corollary the profession of advertising, has led to the re-appearance of the signs, though in many different forms and bearing an emphasis peculiar to the trading conditions of today.

The multiple shop or store of the present century has, by means of standardisation of lay-out, appearance, colour scheme, and even window dressing, impressed its personal and particular characteristics on the minds of the general public. A Woolworth or a Marks and Spencer store, a Lyons teashop, a Boots chemist, Sainsbury provision or Montague Burton tailors' establishment, can all be readily identified, almost subconsciously, by a complete stranger to the particular shopping centre.

Many of these multiples, by means of a standardised sign, draw attention to their presence, such as the S and Sewing Machine of the Singer Company, the blue and white saltire of Macfisheries, or the winged messenger of Achille Serre. Closely linked with these are the trade marks and devices associated with proprietary goods, which appear ever before our eyes, on hoardings and in buses, in magazines, newspapers and shop windows alike.

Many of these trading emblems, slogans or trade marks are so familiar that, were they to appear in an incomplete state or the trade-marks to be devoid of wording, the product would still be identified by the majority. Such symbols as the Sailor of Player's Cigarettes, the Quaker of Quaker Oats, the Dog and Phonograph of His Master's Voice or the famous 57 of Heinz Food Products are all indelibly impressed on our minds by constant repetition.

These trade-marks often appear in the form of a sign given to local traders to display, indicating that they are acting as agents for that particular commodity. The oblong box sign of the Kodak Film, the 'Teas with Hovis' or the Calor Gas Bottle may not have the charm and character of the signs of old but they do fulfil the purpose of the signboard, of identifying a particular shop with a certain trade or commodity.

Another modern trend is to be found in the number of motor vehicles bearing a special sign or enlarged model of a popular product. The Spotted Dog of the Cleaners, the giant packet of Colman's flour, the dog of Spratts' biscuits are typical examples, while in some cases the whole vehicle is specially constructed. The packet of washing powder, the bottle of Worthington, the tube of toothpaste and hundreds of similar examples all act as mobile signs, not drawing attention to any individual shop, but to a certain range of goods.

In some cases, commercial undertakings adopt a particular building as their own trade mark, emblem or sign and in consequence make that building known throughout the land and sometimes throughout the world.

FAMILIAR TRADE-MARKS,
EMBLEMS AND BADGES.

The Three Spires of Coventry for Hillman Motors, the Houses of Parliament on the label of H.P. Sauce, the slender spire of Norwich Cathedral for both the Norvic Shoe Company and the Norwich Union Insurance Societies, and the Castle of Nottingham for John Player and Sons are all examples of this trend.

There exists also a group of signs which are peculiar to this day and age, the products mainly of the motor transport industry. There is the 'L' sign of the various schools of Motoring, who display outside their premises a replica of the red L on a white background, the learner driver's emblem. The Ferguson Tractor Dealers have a sign showing the tractor in silhouette, the Marsham Tyre Company have a Map of the World encircled by a Tyre, National Benzole have the Head of Hermes, and the Michelin Tyre Company have the Michelin Man who is made of tyres.

The invention of neon strip lighting gave added impetus to the advertising signs for it provided not only illumination and colour but movement coupled with visibility over considerable distances. The mammoth bottles pouring out their cascades of golden liquid, the winking eyes and moving figures may be far removed from the signs of the seventeenth century, but they surely are their lineal descendants, and, as such, remind us that in this nation of shopkeepers the Traders' Signs are still a living force and not just a piece of bygone history.

BIBLIOGRAPHY

A Hundred Years of Joint Stock Banking. W. F. Crick and J. E. Wadsworth. Hodder & Stoughton. 1935.

The Early History of Banking in England. R. D. Richards. P. S. King and Son Ltd, Westminster, 1929.

Footprints of Assurance. A. E. Bulan. Macmillan, New York. 1953.

The Guilds and Companies of London. George Unwin. Methuen 1908.

The First Fifty Years. Arthur J. Watson, Municipal Mutual Insurance. 1953.

History of Barclays Bank Ltd. P. W. Matthews and A. W. Tuke. Blades, East and Blades, London. 1926.

Heraldry, Historical and Popular. Charles Boutell. Winsor and Newton. 1863.

The History of Signboards. Jacob Larwood and John Camden Hotten. John Camden Hotten, Piccadilly. 1866.

Insurance Office Signs. Bertram Williams. Insurance Clerks Orphanage. 1929.

London's Livery Companies. Robert J. Blackham. Sampson Low, Marston and Co. Ltd.

National Provincial Bank, 1833—1933. Hartley Withers. National Provincial Bank.

Personal Account. Sir S. H. Scott, Bt. and F. C. Scott. Provincial Insurance Co. Ltd. 1953.

On This Evidence. E. P. Leigh-Bennett. Baynard Press, 1936.

The Stones and Curiosities of Edinburgh and Neighbourhood. G. A. Fothergill. John Orr, Edinburgh. 1910.

The Signboards of Old London Shops. Sir Ambrose Heal. Batsford. 1947.

The Signs of Old Lombard Street. F. G. Hilton Price. Field and Tuer

BIBLIOGRAPHY

The Trade Signs of Essex. Miller Christy. E. Durrant and Co., Chelmsford, 1887.

'Twixt Lombard Street and Cornhill. Lloyds Bank Ltd. 1930.

The Westminster Bank, through a century. T. E. Gregory. Oxford University Press. 1936.

What Inn Signs Tell. Whittoney Block. Imprimerie Mentonnaise. 1929.

The Merchants' Marks in the City of Norwich. W. C. Ewing. Charles Muskett, Norwich. 1850.

Tokens Issued in the Seventeenth Century. William Boyne, London. 1858.

INDEX

INDEX

INDEX

INDEX

INDEX

For Product Safety Concerns and Information please contact our EU representative GPSR@taylorandfrancis.com Taylor & Francis Verlag GmbH, Kaufingerstraße 24, 80331 München, Germany